Memories

of

Stourbridge

The publishers would like to thank the following companies

for their support in the production

of this book

Hayes Tubes Limited

Helix Group plc

Hewitt & Sons Limited

Geoff Hill Limited

Sunfield School

Old Swinford Hospital School

Prospect Coaches (West) Limited

Vee Bee Limited

First published in Great Britain by True North Books Limited
England HX5 9AE

ISBN 1 903204 31 3

Text, design and origination by True North Books Limited
Printed and bound in Great Britain

Introduction

There are many ways to celebrate the past - one often favoured by historians is to concentrate on events which caused great upheaval to communities and detail the activities of the great movers and shakers in world history. Although this is certainly an important perspective, the view of what are often termed 'ordinary people' seems somewhat different. Changes continually come but rarely do they demand overnight alterations in the way we go about our day-to-day lives. Our overall impression is that life goes on smoothly and we gradually assimilate changes as we go along and it is often only when we take time to look back and take stock that we realise just how different our lives are from what they were even ten years ago. In this book we offer the reader the opportunity to do just that. It is not a book of local history in the usual sense, and although the names of the great and the good who have stamped their influence and names on the life of Stourbridge are mentioned in passing, we concentrate on scenes from everyday life which constitute the framework in which all of us live out lives which may not be 'important' in the same way but which nevertheless make a difference to those whose lives connect with ours.

Continued overleaf

From previous page

The history of Stourbridge is a good demonstration of the principle of gradual evolution of activity. We see that the people of Stourbridge have constantly adapted to the changes which came their way, starting with the time the town was simply a convenient crossing place over the River Stour in the Middle Ages (what is now the A491) and a suitable place for holding a weekly market, continuing through the times when, in common with many other communities, woollen cloth production was an important way of earning a living, to the more recent history when the town was connected to the River Severn by canal and to the railway network which opened up vital means of transporting raw materials to the town and finished products to their markets - a critical factor in securing Stourbridge's place as a major contributor to the Industrial Revolution through its iron and glass works.

In this book we offer a taster of Stourbridge life which is within the lifetime of many and it is certainly a fascinating, though random record. We should be grateful for the vision of those who commissioned the Worcestershire Photographic

Survey from which the majority of the photographs in this publication are taken and it is certain that the Archive 2000 project initiated by Dudley Libraries as an appropriate undertaking at the start of a new millennium will furnish us with a similarly fruitful source of memories in years to come.

We hope you will enjoy the book which tells a story written unconsciously by every resident of Stourbridge over the comparatively recent past and which will continue as long as the town exists. The town centre offers so much that is pleasant, even splendid and has the enormous advantage of the amenities of Mary Stevens Park among others. There is a larger than average quota of listed buildings and the establishing of a Conservation Area in the town centre ensures that all that is best from the town's past will be preserved for future generations to enjoy. An increasing number of visitors come to the town by canal boat each year to sample its attractions, but it is chiefly Stourbridge residents themselves who can appreciate the full range of what the town offers. To them we offer a chance to savour and celebrate the importance of the everyday routine events of life.

Contents

Street scenes

A view looking down Market Street, Stourbridge in 1942 from the top of the Midland Bank. The cupola and part of the interesting tower of the Town Hall can be clearly seen. It was built on the site of the Old Corn Exchange to mark the Golden Jubilee of Queen Victoria in 1887 and was considered 'nothing short of a disgrace to the town' by the Stourbridge Commissioners. Funds were obtained by public subscription. It was designed and built by Stourbridge architect Thomas Robinson in red brick and terra-cotta, in the local architectural tradition; his design was chosen out of three submitted by local architects and Robinson's received unanimous approval of the planning committee. A large proportion of the building materials were locally produced. Following the official opening was a lunch attended by 300 people for which tickets were sold which cost 7s 6d for gentlemen and 5s for ladies. A new Corn Exchange, Fire Station, Council Chamber and Council Offices were added the following year. On Market Street now stands the Stourbridge Institute and Social Club which was founded in 1843, 'to afford information on a variety of interesting subjects especially among the labouring classes'. It moved to the present site in 1857 when the Falcon Inn was bought. The original building was extended in the early part of the 20th century. The doorway and the detailing above it form Stourbridge's best example of the Art Deco style popular in the 1920s and 1930s.

How quiet and peaceful everything looks on Stourbridge High Street in this view taken around 1950. It was taken from the Old Library building. Bosworth's shop can be seen on the left, and The Odeon cinema is also visible, it was showing 'The Count' starring Charlie Chaplin. This had previously called The Central when it was opened in 1929 On the right is a Ladies' and Gentlemen's hairdresser's. The 1950s was a time of great optimism, they saw the ending of rationing and people looked forward with anticipation to a new way of life which contrasted sharply with the austerity they had experienced during the war years. There was the prospect of greater prosperity and people now had new expectations.

A company called Dri-Kleen Ltd was established in the High Street about this time and advertised in the local press as follows: Try the Bagwash, Express Service Your family wash done for 3/-. Over 3000 people are sending their weekly wash to the BAGWASH service. You fill a bag with anything that will boil (no lists to write). We wash in soft water and pure soap, it is then damp dried... and returned next day ready to iron. The High Street contributes to the overall attractiveness of the town which has an enviable collection of fine buildings; these have been expertly reproduced in an embroidery collage designed by Jenny Howe and executed by members of Stourbridge's Embroiderers' Guild. It hangs in the foyer of the town library in the Crown Centre, Stourbridge.

Right: This picture was taken from the Old Library which is now a listed building at the junction of New Road, High Street and Hagley Road. In the foreground the War Memorial is in its original position, before the construction of

Bottom: Taken in 1930 next to the Great Western Railway Goods Office, this picture shows the High Street, Amblecote with the bridge over the River Stour. The centre post of the bridge represented the boundary between Amblecote and Stourbridge, marked by a white sign on the

the ring road which necessitated it being removed to the safety of Mary Stevens Park. The sign on the Evesham Fruit Shop on the corner was encouraging folk to 'buy from the growers and save money' and claimed 'everything fresh daily'. The spire of the Church of Our Lady and All Saints rises magnificently 130 feet into the air on the left; it was built in 1889 two years after the new Town Hall had been opened. The 1880s were a time of great expansion and optimism in Stourbridge. In 1880 the railway line was extended to take goods traffic to Stourbridge Town Station and in 1884 the first steam trams began operation from the end of the High Street to Dudley station. In 1885 the Post Office in the High Street was opened, and in 1887 the Methodist School in New Road opened its doors to its first pupils. This was also the year in which the new Town Hall was completed and officially opened. They were superseded in 1899 by the electric tram which were themselves abolished after over thirty years honourable service in 1930.

stonework. Seen here as a peaceful scene, the road was to become a busy thoroughfare and congestion led to the need for its widening. Work on this commenced in 1968 and the bridge was strengthened so it could cope with the volume of heavy traffic it was called on to carry. This work necessitated the demolition of some of the buildings you can see here. The Georgian mansion and estate called The Hill was purchased in 1892 for the sum of ú6,500 by John Corbett to provide hospital accommodation in Amblecote, he also gave an additional ú2,000 for the work necessary to convert a private residence into a hospital. Initially there was a five bed ward for women, a four bed ward for men a six bed accident ward and two small additional rooms, a total of 18 beds. Funding for the running of the hospital relied on the generosity of the local people. For many years the hospital was the only charity supported by Amblecote people. The opening ceremony of the Corbett Hospital was the occasion also for the first Hospital Fete, subsequently an annual event. The band concerts at the fetes were so popular that a bandstand was erected in the hospital grounds in 1903.

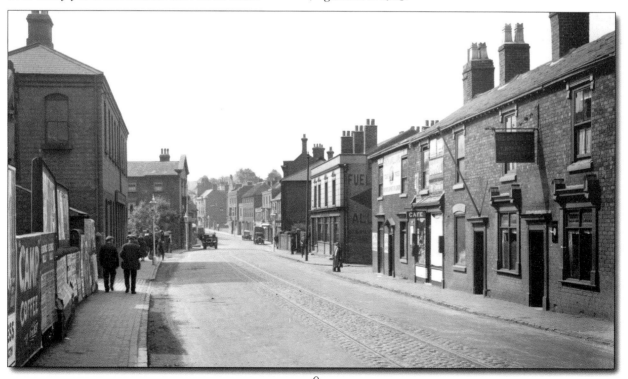

High Street, Stourbridge in 1956. The shop fronts of Marsh & Baxter, Wimbush and Halford's can be seen. The bus is carrying an advert for Bovril. The street presents an attractive scene with a pleasing variety of architectural styles. Businesses located in the High Street advertising their services in the local paper in that year included Geo. Smith (prop. H Giles) at number 54 who sold 'shoes of distinction', among them Clark's, Moccasin, Liberty, church, Start-Rite and Kiltie, and undertook 'repairs of quality'. J Hulme (prop. J W Shaw) was a tobacconist next to the Post

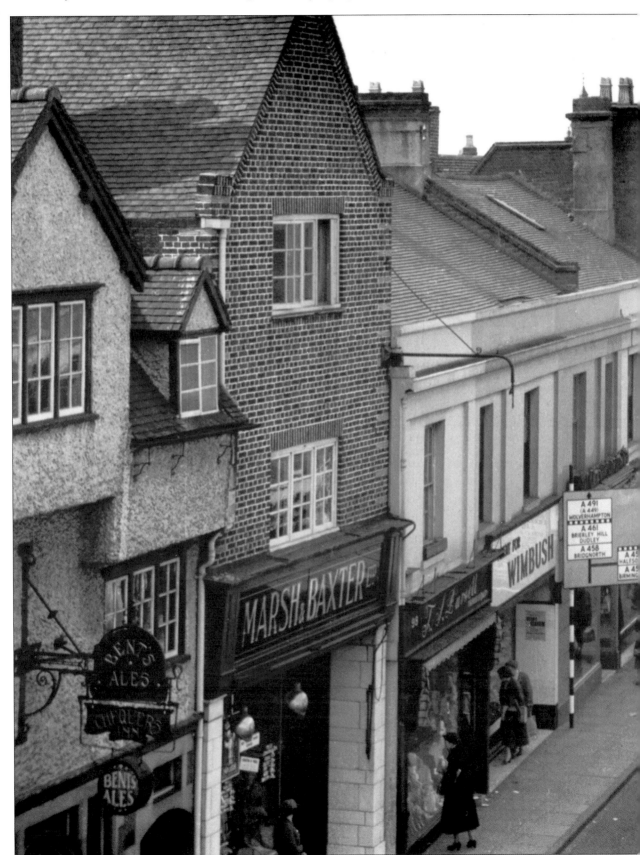

Office, selling 'pipes, pouches, lighters and cigarette cases'. Further down at 165 Lower High Street there was Henry's, permanent waving and tinting specialists, who offered 'treatments' and wigs along with 'a first class service for the woman who appreciates comfort, cleanliness and hygiene', their proud boast was 'instruments sterilised by bacterial process'. The house at 6 and 7 Lower High Street is known as 'Sandford House' and may be considered to be one of the most handsome Georgian residences in the borough. It is so named because it was built near a high sandstone bank around 1770.

Bottom: This unusual view of a very familiar Stourbridge landmark was taken probably before the second world war. The camera is facing down Lower High Street and the Mitre Hotel is in the centre left. The distinctive Dutch gable, which dates from the late seventeenth century, on the building occupied by Nickolls & Perks can be seen in the bottom right hand corner. The rooftops of King Edward VI College can also be seen on the right hand side of Lower High Street. The photograph was taken from the roof of what was the Midland Bank. This very attractive building is presently occupied by the Yorkshire Bank, the words 'Old Bank' are to be found carved in the stonework over the doorway. This view looks somewhat different today since the pedestrianisation of this area but the location is unmistakable. The Crown Shopping Centre was yet to be built when this picture was taken. This junction can reasonably claim to be the centre point of the town being at the place where five roads meet, the High Street, Lower High Street, Crown Lane, Coventry Street and Market Street, not least also as it is the location of the Town Clock. This area is within the boundaries of the Stourbridge conservation area, and on the whole the centre of the town offers an attractive sight for anyone taking the time to appreciate what it has to offer.

Right: The shops on the south side of Bridgnorth Road, Wollaston, taken from opposite Cobden Street as they were in 1959. The one on the corner at the end of the parade is Wilday A Allin, who also had a shop at 153 High Street, Stourbridge. Wollaston is less than a mile from the centre of Stourbridge but a hundred years ago it was still a separate community and was surrounded by fields. A number of streets in this area are named after figures famous for political or socially beneficial deeds. Cobden Street, for example was so called after Richard Cobden (1804-65) the Liberal MP for Stockport. There is also Duncombe Street after Thomas Slingsby Duncombe who was an MP and a champion of the poor. Bright Street commemorates John Bright who was MP for Durham for over 25 years. Important to the locality was John Hatton's spade & shovel works which provided employment for many years until its closure and subsequent demolition shortly after the end of the second world war. Enville Street formed the first part of the main road from Stourbridge to Bridgnorth which passes through Stourton, Kinver and Enville, this became a turnpike in 1816. A waist-high pole spanned the road outside the tollkeeper's cottage - the pole was turned once the toll had been paid.

England. The High Street has often been considered too narrow, for example it was only wide enough to accommodate a single tram track for the service to Stourbridge.

The last tram ran in February 1930.

Top: How wide and spacious the road appears and what a contrast with today's Hagley Road, especially at peak travel times. This photograph was taken looking in the direction of the High Street, Union Street leads off at the left hand side. The Fountain Inn may be seen, as well as Butler's shop. The couple on

Above: High Street, Lye in 1950. This used to be the centre of both social and commercial activity before the coming of the supermarkets, with a wide variety of shops to serve the needs of the local residents. It is still today a thriving community. This picture shows the High Street without a single car in sight, or pedestrians either for that matter, but Lye was not always such a peaceful scene; the General Election in 1874 was the occasion of strong feelings and emotions in Lye, to such an extent that the militia was called out and The Riot act was read, followed by swift action to quell the rioting mob. It is thought that it was the last occasion on which this powers under this Act were used in

the left are wheeling their baby out in a pram equipped with proper springs and a well-insulated body, which must have been so much more comfortable and cosy for the child compared with the convenient fold-up buggies of today - no one has undertaken a survey of those under the age of one to discover consumer opinion on the subject, but babies would probably vote for the model shown here or something like it. However getting this up steps and through revolving doors is another matter, and travel whether by car or public transport would be quite impossible. The large, fringed sun shade on the pram is also a thing of the past.

On the left of this view of High Street, Lye from Lye Cross looking in the direction of Birmingham, in July 1958 is the pub which when first opened was called 'The Crown'. It became known as 'The Rose and Crown' on account of the panel, visible here above the upstairs windows, which showed a rose in relief above a crown. In any case, the pub was known locally as 'Merica Bar' mainly on account of the interior decor. There was a brass footrail at the counter and a horses' hitching rail across the windows in the manner of saloons in America's Wild West. There is no record of it ever having been necessary to call

for the Sheriff to break up gun fights. The Centre Building, Lye Cross was built in 1903. Some of the most noteworthy buildings in Lye still remain, one which is considered to be worthy of mention is Rhodes Building, a three storey edifice constructed of red and yellow brick with terracotta decoration. This once served as an international Public Call Office and held clocks which showed the time in India, Pakistan, Bangladesh and Yemen. The High Street was wide enough to accommodate only a single track tram on which ran a service to Stourbridge, this ran for the last time in February, 1930.

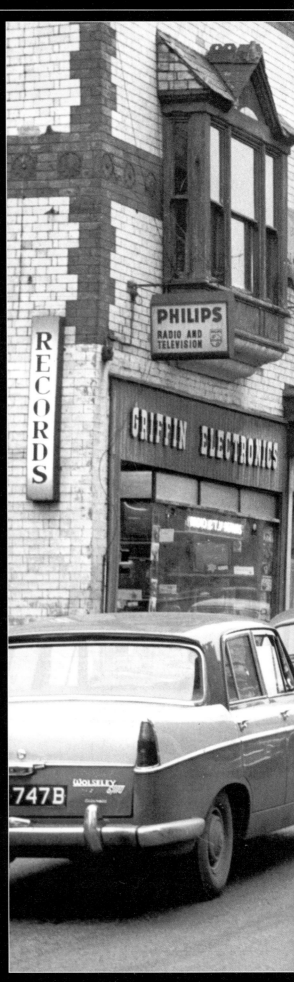

Above: Oldswinford Church taken in 1950. This was the first parish church in Stourbridge. It traces its history back to 1285 and the tower dates from the late 14th century, but the rest of the building is comparatively recent. The magnificent spire was erected in 1810 and removed in 1982. In the church is a monument to James Foster, ironmaster whose ironworks built the 'Stourbridge Lion' and the "Agenoria' and who by employing many local workmen contributed enormously to the wealth of the area. One of the rectors of the parish achieved a certain notoriety by marrying his cook and preaching about it. Oldswinford Parish Rooms were opened in 1906 but after over 60 years were sold and the proceeds used towards the building of the new hall at the east end of the church. St Andrew's Church was built in 1939 to cater for the growing population of the Wollescote area. A new church hall was built at the rear of this and was subsequently remodelled as a new church. The Holy Trinity Church in Amblecote was opened in 1842 and is faced with local firebrick. It cost £4,280 to build, the money having been raised by local business men. A Mission Room was opened in King William Street in 1889 and from the proceeds of the sale of this building a Parish Hall adjacent to the church, was erected in 1922.

The north side of the High Street in Lye as it was in 1966. Clinic Drive runs off to the left. The businesses seen here are Griffin Electronics which sell Philips Radio and TV as well as records, Cath's Cafe, Lloyd's Bank, Melody Jewels and Barclay's Bank. It is a busy scene. The 1960s saw the fulfilment of the dream of those who had suffered the austerity of the second world war and its aftermath of rationing as it was a time a material prosperity. Owners of the Wolseley cars like the one on the left of the picture recall with fondness the days when they enjoyed the roomy interior which offered walnut and leather trim. This year was also the one which saw a 17-year old called Lesley Hornby turn ideas of female beauty upside down with her bobbed hair and waifish look when she came on the fashion scene as 'Twiggy'. This was also the year of the Aberan tragedy when a colliery tip slid into the nearby village, burying the local school as children were settling to their first lessons of the day. The year also witnessed the historic victory of the England football team over West Germany at Wembley, thanks to two goals by Hurst in extra time. The space team of Star Trek also started 'to boldly go where no man has gone before' in 1966. Hits in the charts of that year included, 'The Green, Green Grass of Home' by Tom Jones, 'Strangers in the Night' from Frank Sinatra, 'Yellow Submarine' and 'Eleanor Rigby' from the Beatles.

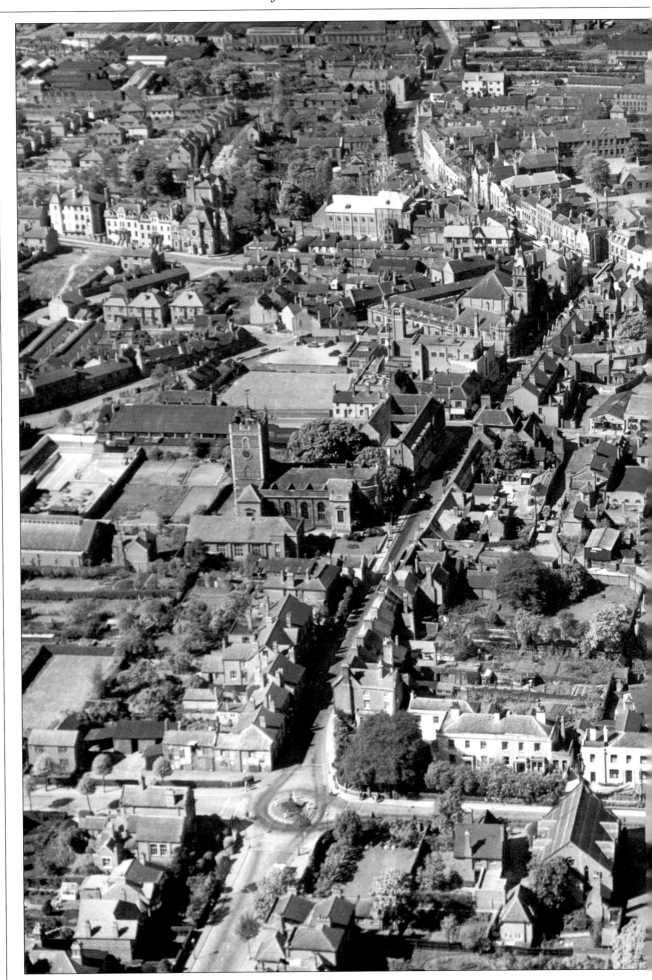

An aerial view of Stourbridge as it was in 1954. The High Street crosses the photo from the right, the Lower High Street snaking away off the top centre and Market Street comes down towards the viewer through the centre of the frame, joining New Road near the bottom of the picture. St Thomas's Church is clearly visible in the middleground centre. This church can reasonably claim to be one of the most beautiful and interesting buildings in a town which has no shortage of such. It was completed in 1728 at a time when Stourbridge was undergoing a period of rapid development with many people coming to live there from the surrounding countryside. The old parish church at Oldswinford was then too far away as well as too small to cater for these people so a new church was felt to be a necessity. for many years it was known as the 'New Chapel' and was without its own parish. The first minister was Walter Hickman, who was self-appointed and took possession of the church without the consent of the trustees, and he was succeeded by four men who also had the duty of Headmaster of the King Edward VI Grammar School. It is of local brick construction and has gone through numerous alterations during its history. In 1859 the simplicity of the interior was changed slightly by the inclusion of stained-glass windows, a favourite with the Victorians. In 1836 in order to accommodate the increasing number of worshippers, galleries were fitted and the original tall box pews replaced.

Left: Here is a view of Pedmore Road, Lye as it looked in 1964. The camera is facing the Grange Lane, Stourbridge direction and shows how things looked before the road widening which took place in August, 1964. The vast increase in car ownership made this a familiar sight across the country at this time. Motorways were also speeding up the flow of traffic (for a time anyway). Mary Poppins was delighting audiences across the country and Mary Quant the fashion designer sported the new hairdo which was to revolutionise women's hairdressing when she had her hair 'bobbed' by Vidal Sassoon, the leading hair-stylist of the time. An innovation which as to transform the lives of typists made its entrance in this year, IBM introduced a machine which displayed the last few words typed on the keyboard giving the opportunity for corrections to be made before the text was printed on the paper - for the first time even incompetent typists could produce faultless letters. By this time large housing estates were being provided by the council and private builders for residents of Lye and Stourbridge as a whole, using land which until then had been fertile farmland. One of the oldest buildings in the old Borough of Stourbridge is the church at Pedmore, rivalling the parish church of Oldswinford in antiquity, remains of a church on the site date from the 12th century.

Above: This photograph was taken around 1962 and shows the south end of Victoria Street, Stourbridge looking from New Road. The row of terraced houses in the centre of the picture has since been demolished to make way for a small car park. Cars have certainly changed the way we live our lives perhaps more than any other, and there is evidence on this picture of their influence. Only fifty years ago there would probably have been no cars at all on a street like this but now there's half a dozen or more, together with a fuel tanker which is now a regular sight on our motorways and trunk roads. Changes in car design can also been discerned - the car behind the lady on the right hand footpath shows its age in terms of its bulky squat shape and forms quite a contrast to the cars on the opposite side of the street which are altogether a different sort of shape. Cars have continued to become more and more streamlined in shape, as the drive for more economical motoring has increased over the years. The car has transformed work patterns also. Once people could work no more than five miles away from home, as a journey on foot would take just over an hour to complete that sort of distance, but in the same time in a car, far greater distances can be travelled.

There are no mini-skirts to be seen in Stourbridge on this particular day but it wouldn't be long before it was the accepted fashion for young and then older ladies. This is how the High Street, Stourbridge looked in 1960. Lloyd's bank may be seen and Stead and Simpson's as well as Hedges, Chemists. The Odeon cinema is also in the picture; this was built in 1929 and was called the Central at that time, becoming the Odeon in 1938; it seated 1,400. Among the films on general release that year was Alfred Hitchcock's 'Psycho' and Fellini's 'La Dolce Vita'. E Blurton, Jewellers, was to be found at 45 High Street, in the local paper around this time they were advertising, 'all fashionable styles and modern designs' and requested, they have 'the pleasure of showing you our selection, prices from £3/15/0. The population of Stourbridge at this time was around 41,000, it had grown steadily from the time the borough was enlarged in 1933 from just over 34,000. In 1960, 669 births and 374 deaths were recorded; housing statistics show there were 384 houses built and 45 demolished during that year. The radio shop pictured on the right was, whether the proprietor knew it or not on the verge of a new era of prosperity as the 1960s saw the opening up of mass communications, and new technology brought ever increasingly complex but at the same time cheaper consumer durables like radios and record players.

A picture of a long-standing feature of Stourbridge town centre taken in the 1950s. The Mitre Inn at the junction of Crown Lane and where High Street becomes Lower High Street. This view looks somewhat different today, having been pedestrianised along with Coventry Street opposite. The sign on the flower bed encourages people to, 'Please keep to the Paths'. A little further down the street on the right hand side King Edward VI School, "The Grammar School' may be seen. This is one the town's oldest institutions. It was the subject of a charter from Edward VI on 17 June 1552 who commanded that 'there should be for ever a Grammar School at Stourbridge'. A famous 'old boy' was Samuel Johnson who attended briefly between 1725 to 1726, he was fifteen years old at the time. There are the initials S J carved on the wainscoting in one of the classrooms and tradition has it that they were carved by him. Of the school, Johnson was to say in later years, 'While at Stourbridge I learned much from the master but little from the school'. The master in question was a certain John Wentworth, of whom Johnson said, 'he was a very able man, but an idle man, and to me very severe'. He was constantly in trouble with the school governors and was dismissed in 1732 for taking an unauthorised extension to the Whitsun holiday. He refused to give up his post, however and continued to occupy the school house and draw his salary until his death in 1740.

Above: Stourbridge High Street as it was in 1965. Marks & Moody's can be seen as well as Yeates Chemist's. Of historic interest is the motorcycle and side-car seen at the bottom right of the picture. Likewise the fine collection of minis parked on the side of the street have become rarer over the years and have recently ceased production to the regret of many who have many happy memories of the travels they undertook in them. This year saw the first attempt by Japanese car manufacturers to break into the British car market. The first onslaught on the formerly secure home car market came with the introduction of the Daihatsu Compagno Berlina saloon.

There aren't any jump-suits in evidence on the High Street as far as we can tell but 1965 was the year they created something of a fashion sensation when they were first seen worn by Diana Rigg in the very popular 'Avengers' Television series. This lace over pink outfit with flared trousers was just the thing for throwing your co-star, in this case Patrick Macnee over your shoulder. This was the time that Carnaby Street in London was the mecca for fashionable, or as they liked to call themselves, 'switched on' people. It marked a radical departure from traditional 'fashion' concepts and introduced an era when style was defined more by the individual than those 'experts'.

This picture shows the town centre landmarks of the Mitre Inn, the Market Hall and the Town Clock and the general view as it looked in the mid 1960s. The clock was constructed locally at J Bradley's Ironworks in 1857, designed by William Millward at the works. The mechanism was originally housed inside the Market Hall, and for many years the clock was wound under contract by a local firm of jewellers and clockmakers who had to climb into the loft of the Market Hall twice a week to accomplish their task. The clock motor was electrified in 1972. In 1989 it was removed its place outside the Market Hall and transported to Bristol to be restored. There was some debate as to where it should be sited after the restoration work had been done, but it was eventually returned to its original position. The Coat of Arms of Stourbridge was not granted until 1917. The background of the shield is blue and has the span of a bridge in silver crossing the centre from left to right. From the bridge hangs a golden fleece on a black chain, above the bridge a pear occupies each of the corners. An official explanation states: the name of the Borough and its close connection with the County of Worcester are symbolised by the bridge and the two Pears, whilst the Fleece and the Chain suspending it are typical of the Skin and Leather Dressing and Chain Cable Industries, carried on in the borough. The motto, 'one heart, one way', expresses the 'singleness of mind and purpose' animating the Members of the Town Council.

At leisure

These happy faces, old and young, belong to a group watching the Punch and Judy Show at the Stourbridge Floral Fete held in Mary Stevens Park in August, 1956. With the wealth of variety of entertainments for children these days it is unlikely that a crowd of this size would be attracted to watch the antics of Mr Punch. But electronic enjoyments were unavailable to these people and they were entering into the enjoyment of all a day out on a lovely summer's afternoon could afford. The Floral Fete was a good opportunity for organisations and companies to show the general public what they were offering as many people attending had the leisure to stop and look and talk. On this picture in the background we see the stands displaying information about the local paper, the 'Express and Star' and doubtless they had at least one reporter out and about in the park that day reporting on all the events and activities. Also visible is a stand detailing the benefits of Electricity which was fast becoming a popular source of fuel for cooking and for domestic heating, taking over from coal. The demand for coal however continued to be strong because, of course, it was needed to generate the electricity which was being promoted so strongly here today. An advert recruiting for the National Coal Board at this time stressed the security which the industry could give, and has the man on the advert stating, somewhat ironically for those who know what was to follow, 'it's obvious that Britain will need more and more coal throughout my whole life'. An additional attraction was the level of pay offered, a minimum of £9 0s 6d per week, a generous holiday allowance and other benefits such as cheap coal and the opportunity to live in a new house owned by the NCB. 'Coal mining is a job for *good*', or so they thought at the time.

A picture of the crowd at Stourbridge Floral Fete, Mary Stevens Park in August 1955. No one looks particularly joyful, perhaps they had been sitting a long time waiting for the entertainment to start. Only the youngest present on this pleasant summer afternoon would have been unaware of Ernest Stevens, Stourbridge's great benefactor to whom they owed the privilege of being able to enjoy the wide open spaces of this park. The site was formerly the Studley Court Estate and he bought the land for £15,000 in 1929 to save it from being divided into building plots. He presented it to the town for use as a public park and commissioned the impressive entrance gates . The park was opened by him on 6 April 1931, he named it Mary Stevens Park in memory of his wife who had died in March 1925. After this ceremony he received the honorary Freedom of the Borough in recognition of his generous gift. Ernest Stevens' liberality sprang from his conviction that wealth was a sacred trust to be used for the benefit of all; this donation of parks appealed to him as he wanted to benefit children and provide peaceful spots for the elderly. His fortune was acquired in business in which he demonstrated rare acumen and organising ability. He was known locally as 'Bucket King' as his firm made hollow-ware at the Stour Vale Works in Cradley Heath.

Bottom: It is high summer, 1951 but, yes, these children are carrying toboggans up to the top of Clent Hill. This out of season sport was in fact aided by the hot weather which had dried the surface of the grass until it was more slippery then pressed snow. Resident Edward Davis of Mount Hill Cottage, Clent felt that the tourist spot had been losing its appeal over recent years and decided to do something about it. He made each one of the toboggans pictured here and several more besides - 165 in all. They were substantial enough to take the pounding they would receive from the youngsters having been made of oak or ash. Mr Davis charged 6d per hour for the hire of them for the ride down the 150 yard slope and they proved extremely popular - there were up to 500 children taking advantage of this opportunity on some Sundays. It was an extremely enjoyable experience for them, as high speeds were possible. Accidents were rare and none were serious because of the robust construction materials and the fact that participants had to lie down on the toboggan and were then only two inches off the ground. This sounds like an absolutely ideal recreation but unfortunately it suffered from numerous thefts, as some motorists took them home with them at the end of the day. There was also another hazard - the nearby location of a pool of water, in which many toboggans found their way. The enterprising Mr Davis solved this by training his three dogs to retrieve them.

Right: These four are enjoying a day out in the Clent Hills in April, 1952. This local beauty spot is deservedly popular with locals who appreciate the opportunity to take a healthy walk in the countryside, and the chance to admire the view from the top of the hills. Though a great deal of building has taken place in the years since this picture was shot, the Clent area still lays claim to being 'out in the country'.

The way we spend our leisure time had changed dramatically since the second world war. Increased wealth coupled with shorter working hours has resulted in more time available for leisure activities and a massive growth in the range of shops available; we have seen the growth during the last thirty years or so of huge shopping malls, great cathedrals to celebrate consumerism. Stourbridge boasts its own shopping centres, the Rye Market and the Crown Centre. However it is the Merry Hill Centre to the north of the town which has had a dramatic effect on the way people have shopped since the first stage of development opened in 1985. Such developments are always controversial as the often mutually exclusive demands of creating employment, satisfying consumer demand and conservation of sites important for flora and fauna compete for prominence in the public consciousness and perhaps more importantly in the minds of those with the responsibility for decision making. In addition to all the other complications such developments are bound to have certain implications for the profitability of the businesses in the surrounding towns.

These girls are taking part in the ceremonies associated with the opening of the new church hall of St Michael's and All Angels' church on the Norton Estate, Stourbridge. The commemorative stone seen here at the bottom left of the picture was officially laid by The Lord Lieutenant of Worcestershire (Admiral Sir William Tennant), then afterwards 600 local school children also played their part by giving the stone a symbolic tap. The girls seen on the photo are just a few of those children. St Michael's and All Angels, Norton was known at first as St Thomas's Mission church and met originally in a corrugated iron structure. Early in 1951 it ceased to be a daughter church when Norton became an ecclesiastical district in its own right formed from parts of St Thomas's and Oldswinford parishes. The Mother Church of the Borough is St Mary's Oldswinford. A church existed on this site in 1285, but the building that stands here today has a tower which was built in the late 14th century, the nave from 1842 and the chancel from 1898. The Roman Catholic community had a tiny chapel in Stourbridge in 1820, but about that time there was a substantial migration of Irish families to the district and work began on a new chapel in New Road. This was replaced by the present Church of Our Lady and All Saints in 1864 with the 130 foot spire which dominates the Stourbridge skyline, added in 1889. Stourbridge has also been home to numerous Nonconformist congregations, the most noted building belonging to such must be the Methodist church in New Road which was opened in June 1928 at a cost of over £13,000.

Ah, aren't they cute? The three babies and two toddlers who are the cause of a lot of cooing among the assembled crowd and pride in the hearts of their parents and grandparents are the winners of the Baby Show Competition held in Mary Stevens Park on the occasion of the Stourbridge Floral Fete in August 1954. How different babies and children were dressed then compared with now. The little boy looks very smart but was not suitably dressed for running around the park - but perhaps he wouldn't have been allowed to; and the little girl is wearing a dress which nowadays is not a usual item of female clothing for everyday use. These children were all members of the generation designated 'Baby Boomers' because of the large number of them - they were the first generation to be born after the conflicts and austerity of the second world war. Their parents had great hopes for them and felt that the increasing wealth becoming available would guarantee them a happy life; however this generation was reaching their late teens and early twenties during the 'flower power' era and many rejected what they considered the 'empty materialism' of their parents, a striking example of the different ideals of different times.

Above: The Old Vine Inn which was in the process of being transformed into the HQ for the Stourbridge Scouts and Guides in 1951. . The opening ceremony after its change of use was performed by Viscount Cobham of Hagley Hall. The Scouts and Guides had had a long search for suitable premises, and it was a chance remark made by a solicitor to the governors of King Edward VI's School which set off the chain of events which led to them purchasing this building. A gift of £250 from Alderman P Jones enabled structural repairs to the half-derelict ex-pub to be carried out. Everything else, remaking of walls, wall-papering, painting, rewiring and the installation of new fire grates was accomplished by scouts and guides in their spare time. here two Guides with the Warden are putting finishing touches to the assembly room which was originally two bedrooms. Nickolls & Perks at the junction of Lower High Street and Coventry Street was called the Board Inn from 1797 till 1968, but it had been used as a private residence before then. A meeting house for Dissenters was built behind it in 1698 but it was burned down by rioters in 1715. The Dutch gables are from the late 17th century. Further down, 164-168 Lower High Street are good examples of two-tone brickwork, fashionable in Victorian times.

Right: Anyone fancy a dip? The light airy swimming pool looks very inviting on what was obviously a bright sunny day in 1956. The girls in the pool are wearing swimming caps which was often compulsory in public baths at the time, but now no longer. Some lads are sizing up the drop into the pool from the diving board which gives them the opportunity to jump from ever-increasing heights in accordance with their experience and nerve. Notice the wire baskets containing the swimmers' clothes, these were the latest thing at the time - many readers will recall the days of the changing cubicles situated on the pool side. There had been a proposal for swimming baths in Stourbridge as long ago as 1886. The idea was revived when the town was considering commemorating Queen Victoria's Diamond Jubilee, and as a result land was bought at the rear of St Thomas's Church. Plans were drawn up and in August 1900 the foundation stone was laid by the chairman of the Council. The baths were opened in May 1901. A fine open-air swimming bath was opened on an adjoining site in 1923. The indoor baths were extended in 1939 at a cost of £28,000. Prior to 1967, the indoor bath was covered during the winter months and used as a hall but afterwards was used for swimming all the year round. The baths closed in 1987 and the Crystal Leisure Centre opened on the same site after public debate about its controversial design in March 1990.

It's 5 November, 1957 outside Ye Olde White Harte Inn in Kinver and a mock execution of a remarkably realistic Guy Fawkes is taking place, providing a deterrent to any there who were contemplating blowing up the Houses of Parliament. Kinver had been built up and prosperous on account of the iron workings there, but it was tourism which boosted the local economy after that industry's decline. It was the Kinver Light Railway was a tramway which brought hundreds of Black Country people into the district on day outings. The Kinver Light Railway was actually an electric tramway four-and-a-quarter miles long which opened on Good Friday, 1901. It was an instant success, chiefly due to the fact that it used the 3'6" gauge which meant it connected with the Black Country Tram network and provided a means for town-dwellers to experience the attractions of this pretty Staffordshire village. So popular did it become that serious overcrowding became a big problem for the operators. In fact at Whitsun 1903 there was a fatal accident on the line when a car licensed for 52 passengers came to grief carrying 80. One person was fatally injured when he fell from the tramcar and fractured his skull. Rules were tightened up and the Railway continued to operate and draw crowds. New Century films made a promotional film to be shown in Black Country cinemas, the result of this was that during the Whitsun holiday period of 1905 over 31,000 passengers were carried on the railway.

Above: How many readers remember the days captured for us on this photograph? Days when there were still streets in Stourbridge where you could walk in the middle of the road without extreme danger. Present day pedestrian precincts give us something of the same feeling, but somehow it's not quite the same as dawdling down a 'proper street'. The date is 1955 and there is still the old gaslight in New Street, Stourbridge. These children look as though they are on their way home from school.

Top: This smart and orderly procession is of boys from Oldswinford Hospital School in 1956 - they are on their way to St Mary's church nearby. Old Swinford Hospital was founded in 1667 by Thomas Foley, the ironmaster to provide education for 60 boys from Stourbridge and certain surrounding parishes. The original school building is still in use today though many new additions have been necessary over the years. Thomas Foley granted the income from several manors and lands to be put at the disposal of the Governors (known as Feoffees) of the school. This enabled the school to give free education and maintenance to needy boys for more than 250 years; in addition a number of extensions to the school including the Maybury Block were funded from this source.

Left: A winter's afternoon in 1956 in Mary Stevens Park, perhaps those walking there are appreciating the wide open spaces and the proportions of the Council House standing majestically in the sunshine. This splendid property was formerly known as Studley Court before it became the Council House in the 1930s. This Georgian Mansion had over the years been home to a number of important local industrialists, including the Rufford family who owned refractories and glass-making works, the Cochranes who were ironfounders, the Turneys, leather dressers and the Webbs, seed merchants. During the first world war Studley Court was used as a military hospital for convalescing servicemen to stay. The religious order of St Andrews took over the Court in 1923 and it became a boarding school for girls. It was put up for sale in 1929 and bought and presented to the people of Stourbridge by local benefactor Ernest Stevens. The parkland was laid out as 'a place of rest for the weary, of happiness for the children, and of beauty for everyone'. The house was restored and a new office wing and council chamber, designed by the Borough Surveyor Frederick Woodward were opened in 1937. There had been opposition to the project when it became known that it would cost £12,000. In March, 1949 the planting of trees in the park to commemorate each Mayor of the borough was begun.

Below: This junior Indian Chief is practising his canoeing skills on South Road Pond. He was in the park with some of his classmates from Stambermill School who had actually constructed it. It is certainly a fine-looking craft and no doubt some watching from the edge are eagerly awaiting their own turn with the oar. Stambermill grew on account of the fireclay which was abundant in the area, which made it an ideal location for brick and retort works. The Oxford, Worcester and Wolverhampton railway line, which opened in 1852, passes over the River Stour on the viaduct at Stambermill. The present brick built viaduct with ten arches was completed in 1882 by Kellett and Bentley at a cost of £13,835. It replaced a wooden trestle style viaduct, built on brick pillars. Traces of the brick foundations still survive. As well as the old Oxford, Worcester and Wolverhampton line, the Stourbridge extension to the G.W.R. line travelling north-eastwards in the Birmingham direction also passes through the locality.

Events & occasions

A **bove:** The man facing the camera in the centre of the picture of a wine tasting at Rutland's vaults in 1956 is the coroner of the time, B G Evers. E Rutland & Son were a feature of the High Street in Stourbridge for a good long time; they occupied Bordeaux House. A good indication of their activities can be gained from an advertisement for the company in the 'County Express' in January, 1956 which states, ' E Rutland & Son, family wine merchants. Bottlers of Bass, Worthington, Watney and Younger Ales, Guinness Harp Label Stout, Bulmers, Evan, Symons and Whyteways Cyder'. The results are displayed on the shelves behind the guests pictured here. Crates bearing the legend, E Rutland & Son, Stourbridge are piled to the

ceiling in the centre. In common with the national trend there are far fewer local breweries in the area than there used to be. The beginnings of a local brewing tradition in the Black Country can be traced to the genius of William Butler who was born in Wolverhampton in 1810. He was apprenticed as an iron worker at Thorneycroft Works, but set up a small grocer's shop as a sideline. He started brewing for the benefit of his customers in 1840 and within two years this side of his business was so successful that he relinquished the grocery shop to brew full time. The popularity of the ales continued to grow and in 1853 he opened his own taproom. He built his own brewery at Grimstone Street, Wolverhampton in 1874 where it operated under the Butler name until it was taken over by Bass.

The distinguished guest performing the official opening of Smarts Furnishing Store in Eagle House on Stourbridge High Street is Anne Crawford. She is carrying a large bouquet of flowers which was in vogue at the time. The notice in the top right hand corner of the picture has a child saying, 'Mum and Dad say they get absolutely everything for our home at SMARTS - on simply wizard terms'. This was the very early days of consumer credit as people responded to the new optimism which emerged when the end of rationing became a realistic prospect and there was increased wealth once the economy had recovered from war-time restrictions. It was the year of the Festival of Britain held on the South Bank of the Thames. It was opened by the King and Queen at the beginning of May of that year and was an immediate success. Londoners flocked to it in their thousands and people from all over the country, indeed all over the world came too. A symbol of the spirit of new hope felt at that time was the long 'Skylon' positioned on the South Bank; at night it was illuminated from within and appeared to hang in the sky with no visible means of support. Earlier Christian Dior had given his first fashion collection which proved instantly popular. His style favoured long flowing dresses and after the sparse fashions of the war the dress needing 50 yards of material represented a new mood of opulence and glamour.

Patricia Cox at Ludlow Bros, Lye in December, 1956. Evidently some new machinery or other development of the business was being celebrated by the presence of such a glamorous person at the works. She is operating the tool which is putting the finishing touches to a dustbin which bears the prestigious 'kitemark' of the British Standards Institution, demonstrating the product conformed to the standards laid down at the time. The contrast between the impeccably turned-out celebrity in all her finery and the workmen in their working clothes could hardly be more striking and no doubt her visit provided a topic of animated conversation for some time afterwards. But life was not all work in Lye, there was the Picture Theatre in the High Street which later became the Victoria cinema, known as 'The Vic' to the locals. In addition to the showing of films here, plays and wrestling matches were also put on for the entertainment of the people of Lye. Cinema sensations of that year included the film adaptation of Jules Verne's 'Around the World in Eighty Days', starring David Niven and Shirley Maclean.

Below: Head Postmaster, Capt J A Cross looks on as the Mayor handles a batch of sorted letters at the Stourbridge Sorting Office in December 1956. These letters have been gathered from one of the bags held open by the frame visible in the foreground, each is labelled with a general sorting area- Wolverhampton, Brierley Hill, Dudley and Stourbridge. The Lady Mayoress looks very fine and warmly dressed against the December weather in her fur coat and leather gloves. What were the thoughts of the sorting office staff, we wonder? Perhaps they were pleased to have a bit of a break in the normal routine, a pleasant interlude before they were plunged into the frenzied activity of the Christmas card season. In the early part of the 19th century, the Post Office at Stourbridge was situated in Crown Lane but later it moved to Lower High Street which was then the business quarter of the town. In 1885, the Post Office moved to High Street and was built on the site of some ancient shops. The garages and yard at the rear occupied the site of the Alhambra, said to have been the last wooden theatre in England. The theatre was pulled down in the late 1920s. An extensive scheme of reconstruction of the High Street Post office was opened on 10 September, 1962 by the then Mayor (Ald J Griffiths).

Bottom: The date is Tuesday, 25 September, 1956 and the occasion is the visit to Stourbridge of the Band of the Grenadier Guards. We see them here standing outside the King's cinema on New Road. They marched to Mary Stevens Park accompanied by three contingents of cadets, where the Mayor and Mayoress (Alderman and Mrs H S Walker) took the salute. Crowds of people turned out to see them, gathering particularly in New Road and Worcester Street. The roads were kept free from traffic by the police, their number swollen for the occasion by Special Constables. In charge of operations was police Superintendent C A Saull, who had himself been a Guardsman. There was a good crowd at the bandstand who enjoyed the hour-long concert given by the band. Afterwards the Mayor invited the band members to the Mayoral Parlour. In the evening they had a meal at the Old White Horse Inn at which Alderman Walker presented a pint tankard to the Director of Music who immediately gave it to the oldest band member - this was quickly followed by the presenting of a half-pint tankard to the youngest member of the band.

Above: The members of the Stourbridge Branch of the Licensed Victuallers' Association pose outside the Assembly Hall in October, 1954. The variety of expressions is probably a good reflection of prevailing attitudes of the time. On the one hand, it was scarcely a decade since the end of the second world war with all the horror that entailed - many of these men would have seen active service. On the other hand there was the distinct prospect of better times ahead - rationing ended in the July of that year and there was a new mood of optimism in the air. These men would have served their customers with beers that were in the main locally brewed as this was the time before the rise of brewery giants. During this year also there was a new drink on the market, this one totally non-alcoholic. In fact there was nothing new about coffee drinking, but it was the scale of its promotion that was new in what had been primarily a tea-drinking society. Coffee bars opened right across the country, and even old-fashioned establishments like The Parisien Grill in London purchased the expresso machines to cater for the demand from customers.

Right: Patients at Prestwood Sanatorium display their 'Guy' in November, 1957. Such institutions were once commonplace but have since become unnecessary as the disease TB has gone into a massive decline. In July the 'County Express' reported the official opening of a mass radiography unit in the Stourbridge area, it was a mobile x-ray unit and planned to visit a canteen of the County Secondary Modern School in Kinver, making a visit to it as convenient as possible for the locals; it was measures like this which contributed to a raising of general health standards in the years following the second world war. Prestwood was later converted into a nursing home. The men here have chosen to make a Sputnik 'Guy', complete with hammer and sickle detail to represent the USSR, a very topical allusion as the Soviets had launched the first satellite into an orbit of the earth only a month before, beating the USA in the space race. Sputnik was given the political impetus (and hence the cash) required when Krushchev, the Soviet premier wanted a propaganda coup to convince a sceptical world that the USSR had developed intercontinental missiles. Just days before this photograph was taken Sputnik II went into orbit carrying a dog called 'Laika' - this was an experiment conducted to assess the effects of space travel on an animal in preparation to making the first manned flights.

Special areas had been reserved in Mary Stevens Park for school children on this special day - April 23, 1957. Perhaps those in charge had wanted to give them the opportunity to get a good view of the Queen and the Duke of Edinburgh who were due to ride past, or perhaps they wanted all the boisterousness concentrated in one place, we may never know. This roadway was later named, appropriately, Queen's Drive. The Cub Scouts seem to be behaving themselves so far, however, even though that may be because they are under the watchful eyes of the Scout Leaders nearby, but they are all dutifully wearing their caps and most are sitting cross-legged. They probably have still plenty of time to wait before the excitement begins as there is quite a number of people standing on the royal route and it is merely the photographer who is causing some people to look this way and smile. The Parks Department had been working very hard to prepare for the occasion and as well as presenting the outdoor areas of the park in the best possible condition, they had furnished the Council House in the park with an abundance of plants and flowers to decorate the rooms the royal party would visit.

Continued overleaf

From previous page.
Above: This was a day to remember for those occupying the special seating provided for these invited guests repre- senting various activities in the town, and no less so for others standing at the rear. Still others are taking advantage of the hillside to obtain a good vantage point to view the royal progress through Mary Stevens Park on this bautifully sunny day. Filling the air with stirring music emanating from the bandstand, is the band of the Gloucestershire Regiment under the direction of Bandmaster G Plummer.

Above right: Crowds have turned out to see the royal couple and the overall mood is one of joyful respect. They were on their way to the Council House to see an exhibition of items made over three centuries of Stourbridge glass production, which had been presented to the town by John Northwood and Benjamin Richardson. The collection had been officially opened May 1952. One other person presented to her Majesty on this occasion was Rev H H Daws, vicar of St John's, Stourbridge who, before coming to the town had founded the Oji River Leper Colony in Nigeria, which the Queen had visited in 1955. The policemen on duty get the best view along with the members of the uniformed organisations - how proud the Girl Guides and Brownies must have felt to be stationed so near to the royal party; the older girls no doubt had instructions to keep an eye on the younger ones. Their majesties were presented with a set of stemmed glasses made by staff and students at Stourbridge College to mark the occasion.

On 26 Sept, 1965 a coach crashed into the front of a cottage on the left hand side of Heath Lane, Old Swinford between Old Swinford traffic lights and Corser Street. The house owners were uninjured as far as we know. The local breakdown garage, Fildes Ltd are on the spot to tow away the erring vehicle, though the main activity in the photograph seems to be standing and viewing. The little girl in the centre has obviously seen more than enough already and is pleading with her Dad to take her home. The coach involved had mounted the pavement and hasn't a single wheel on the road, substantial repair work if not complete demolition will probably necessary as the structural damage (see the loft space) is considerable. Hayes Coaches Ltd operated a fleet of luxury coaches at this time from Lye's Falcon Garage. They carried parties on their annual trips and outings to such seaside resorts as Blackpool, Colwyn, Bay , Llandudno and Rhyl. Smiths of Lye (transport) Ltd was the leading local road haulage concern at this time - it had started out in 1931 when it owned only four wheel lorries, but at this time had a fleet of articulated lorries capable of carrying loads up to 20 tons. Am important component of its business was transporting heavy forgings from local forges across the country and to all leading ports. The well-known Midland Red buses was formed in 1904 and at the time of the photo was the largest bus undertaking in Britain. It operated local services and also long distance express routes across the country.

This rather startling picture was taken in October, 1957, at the time the railway bridge in Foster Street was under reconstruction. here we see the main reason for the work; it was too low for commercial traffic and numerous accidents of this sort occurred as a result. The entire superstructure of the vehicle has been pushed back and very badly damaged. The improvements to the bridge at an estimated cost of £30,000 involved widening the road and lowering it to give greater

clearance under it. The lorry was carrying goods made by the Sunbeam Electric Company, which it claimed were 'the best electric appliances made'. On the left the Bisto kids are savouring the aroma of imaginary gravy, as they continue to do. Bisto was one of the first kitchen cupboard items which offered a short cut way to preparing traditional food, before its advent, gravy making had been a much more complicated and time consuming task. The product started a trend which has continued relentlessly to this day.

On the move

Above: The new bridge at Foster Street, Stourbridge, which was opened on 14 June 1958. The picture was taken facing the direction of High Street. The street was named after James Foster. Both the famous locomotives 'Stourbridge Lion' and 'Agenoria' were built at these works. The Stourbridge Lion was the first locomotive to run on rails in the USA. The Agenoria was used on the Shutt End Railway. The first railway station in Stourbridge was built in Junction Road in May 1852 when the line between Stourbridge and Evesham was opened. This line was part of the old Oxford, Worcester and Wolverhampton railway and was known locally as the 'Old Worse and Worse' as it had a reputation for accidents and mishaps. The Junction Road station and the Town Station in Foster Road were linked together in the 1870s by a track which extended to the Goods Station in Amblecote. This Goods Station was enlarged and provided with office accommodation in 1895. The present Junction Station at Oldswinford was opened in 1901.

The Bus Station in Vauxhall Road, Stourbridge taken from the footbridge to Town Station in 1959. The site of the original Town (Railway) Station is underneath this. The new station was built nearby which makes it a convenient point for travel connections. The tram service in Stourbridge began to be operated by the Dudley and Stourbridge Steam Tramway Co in 1884. In 1889 it was superseded by the electric tram, but trams disappeared completely in 1930. After this the Midland Red Omnibus Co started to operate a service to Stourbridge. The Centro station makes and attractive contribution to the overall appearance of the town, being of a locally relevant design. The Glassblower sculpture situated in the station provides a reminder of one of the major industries connected with the town. At the time this picture was taken there was still the Goods Yard nearby; this was closed down in 1965 and now industrial units occupy the site. The Church of St John the Evangelist, the spire of which is such a prominent landmark on the Stourbridge skyline, is nearby. This was built in 1861 at a cost of about £4,000. The architect was George Edmund, who also designed the Law Courts in the Strand in the City of London.It is of sandstone with a slate roof. The St. John's parish room was opened in 1929 and in 1960 a new church hall costing abut £7,000 was opened. The population of Stourbridge at this time was around 40,500. In 1960 there were 669 births and 374 deaths recorded in the Borough.

This picture was taken in 1965 towards the end of the age of steam. It shows the engine pushing goods up the line towards Brettell Lane Station. It shows the viaduct on Birmingham Street, Stourbridge, looking from Stepping Stones Road seen in the foreground. The line shown here is part of the old Oxford, Worcester and Wolverhampton line which linked Stourbridge to the rail network in 1852. The viaduct itself is quite a feature of Stourbridge's surroundings. The tram service began to be operated by the Dudley and Stourbridge Steam tramway Coin 1884. In 1899 the electric tram superseded it, but the last tram ran in Stourbridge were finally abolished in 1930. In 1905 the Great western railway began a motor bus service between Stourbridge, Clent and Belbroughton. The 'Midland Red' Omnibus Co Ltd., began their service to Stourbridge just after the first world war when buses began to replace the trams. A large garage and bus depot was opened in July 1926 in Foster Street and the Vauxhall Road depot was opened in 1948. An advert for Midland Red in the 'County Express' for July, 1956 offered the attractions of 'no redundancy or short time working in the bus industry; free travel to and from work on company vehicles, good rates of pay, open-air life, up to 18 days PAID HOLIDAY and good training allowances'. They were hoping to recruit drivers conductors and conductresses.

Below: Another steam locomotive is crossing the old bridge in Foster Street in December 1957 before the bridge was raised to provide additional and much-needed clearance for traffic passing underneath it. From the picture it can be seen that the headroom at the time was a mere 11'5" - this was the time when there was a vast increase in traffic of all sorts on the roads and there was pressure to maximise the possible pay-load of lorries in order to cut down on journeys made. The steam locomotive has special connections with Stourbridge . The 'Stourbridge Lion' and the 'Agenoria' were both built at the works of Foster, Rastrick & Co. in Stourbridge. The 'Lion' was the first locomotive to run on a commercial railway in the Americas, and the 'Agenoria' was the first to run to the British Midlands, a full year before the opening of the Liverpool and Manchester Railway. Foster, Rastrick & Co had been major ironfounders and manufacturers and Rastrick had been building locomotives for Richard Trevithick from 1808. in spite of the impressive start to locomotive manufacture made by the company only two other engines were ever produced at the works, these were called the 'Delaware' and the 'America'. The 'Stourbridge Lion and Agenoria Trail' was opened in Canal Street, Stourbridge to celebrate the building of the famous locomotives in 1829. Foster Street which the bridge in the picture crossed was named after the Foster of Foster, Rastrick & Co.

Bottom: Lycett's garage on St John's Road as it was in 1959. They are agents for Humber, Hillman, Sunbeam and Commer - a reminder of when the British car industry was in better shape than at present and when there were several small companies catering for particular markets before the days when they were amalgamated into British Leyland. The young man in the centre of the photo is looking longingly at one of the models in the showroom, possibly wondering if he would ever be able to afford to purchase anything like the gleaming vehicle he could see there. In July 1956 Lycetts had advertised a car newly on the market as follows ; 'Today's finest value in six seater luxury cars - the Humber Hawk, now only £650 (formerly £715) plus purchase tax of £358 17s 0d. Overdrive, white-

wall tyres available as extras. Two-tone colour schemes extra on standard saloon. A Rootes product.' You could fill up your car with Regent petrol in those days. 1959 was the year that the 'bubble' cars were first seen on British streets. They were popular with those finding it hard to park on increasingly busy streets. They had three wheels and were surprisingly stable, but not easy to get out of in a graceful fashion. The prototype of the hovercraft also made its debut in that year - its innovative design employed a cushion of air underneath the craft which enabled it to travel over water faster than conventional ships.

Left: The date is February 1959 and this picture shows the east side of Market Street from the Bell Hotel. This was, naturally enough originally the site of the town's market, which was first held in 1486 on the site of what is no the forecourt of the Crown Centre. It was badly sited, however being accessed by very narrow roads, so that traders often blocked the road and hindered the progress of traffic through the town. This became worse and worse as the town's population increased and it soon became essential that a new market hall be built. The demolition of the old market in 1773 raised hopes that there would soon be a new one in its place but fifty years were to elapse before this was actually realised. Although the site of the new market was close to where the old one had been, it caused far less traffic congestion, as it was in the space between Smithfield, Crown Lane, which was widened for the purpose and what is now Market Street. In the intervening period trading continued with the Smithfield area being used by horse traders and butchers and corn dealers using Rye Market. The street only became known as Market Street in the second half of the nineteenth century. The 'Woodbines' advertised on the shop in the foreground may not now be available but Wall's ice cream and Radio Times continue to be bought in the twenty-first century.

Above: A picture which shows the east side of Worcester Street from Market Street in February 1959. A double-decker bus is travelling up the A451 to Kidderminster , the A491 to Bromsgrove and the A450 to Worcester lead off to the left. The road appears very wide and the trees create a nice suburban atmosphere. The Victorian terraces on the left were probably built in the days when Stourbridge was undergoing rapid expansion occasioned by the coming of the railway. There are at least three cyclists in the photograph and they are not experiencing any of the problems suffered by present day cyclists. They do not need to wear helmets as cycling was not the hazardous occupation it now is. They certainly do not need masks to screen out toxic exhaust fumes from the air they are breathing and they are not forced into the side of the road by extremely high volumes of motor traffic - altogether a very pleasant way of getting about town. The huge increase in the volume of traffic has made a ring road necessary around Stourbridge as well as round numerous other towns, large and small across the country. In common with other towns considerable controversy was stirred up by the building of this, for while it did what it was supposed to do and took through traffic around the town, thus easing congestion on town centre roads, it did in a way isolate the town on an island surrounded by fast moving cars and lorries.

An interesting collection of vehicles in the car park of the local beauty spot of Clent Hills in 1950. Motor cycles with and without side-cars are in evidence but the majority of vehicles are cars on what was probably a summer's weekend and the cars occupants had come to take lungfuls of fresh air and exercise in the pretty Worcestershire countryside. Perhaps they would end an enjoyable day out at the pictures in the evening. Hollywood released 'Sunset Boulevard' starring Gloria Swanson and William Holden and Elizabeth Taylor played Spencer Tracey's daughter in the year's comedy smash, 'Father of the Bride'. James Stewart was upstaged by an invisible rabbit in the film version of the successful stage play 'Harvey'. In November 1950 Ingrid Bergman married the Italian director Roberto Rossellini less than a month after her divorce from her estranged husband causing a scandal. Of more immediate interest to the visitors to Clent Hills would have been the end of soap rationing which happened in the September of that year. Stourbridge is well placed in that it is within easy reach of a number of different types of countryside, from the Vale of Evesham to the south and the Malvern Hills to the south-west. Stratford-upon-Avon and the historic cities of Hereford and Worcester are also relatively close.

Shopping spree

A rather serene picture taken from the roof of what is now the Yorkshire Bank at the bottom of the High Street and shows the market Hall in the bottom left hand corner of the photo. Stourbridge first gained a market in 1486 after Henry VII granted a licence to Earl Ormond in gratitude for his services in the War of the Roses. This market stood where the Crown centre now stands, and was used as the Town Hall, but access to it was not good and in 1773 it was demolished and a new market opened between Smithfield, Crown Lane and Market Street. The building of this however ran into difficulties and it took fifty years before a new market place was ready. The Market Hall building was opened in October, 1827

having cost £20,000 to build. Amblecote timber merchant, John White from Holloway End was the builder. It was originally surrounded on three sides by thoroughfares known as The Shambles which were used by poulterers and butchers. The Market Hall served the townsfolk of Stourbridge well for the next 150 years, originally specialising in fruit and vegetables but eventually selling a wide variety of goods. In the 1980s plans were drawn up by Dudley's planning committee to demolish the Hall but in response to protests from residents and conservation groups it was agreed to retain the facade, preserving this well-loved feature of the town for future generations. The building is now listed ensuring that its future is protected.

The owners of this striking and attractive Stourbridge building are the Rutland family. It is Bordeaux House at the junction of High Street and Foster Street. It was built in terracotta which is very characteristic of the local building style. The ornate second floor has subsequently been removed, detracting from the original appearance. The shop front declares the occupants to be Wine Shippers and the fact that they have a Bonded Warehouse in Dudley. In fact their reputation in the town has been for their selection of wines from abroad, especially France - perhaps this is why their premises were designated Bordeaux House in recognition of one of the most famous wine producing areas of that country. They also undertook bottling of numerous beers brewed by some of the big name breweries which they then made available to their patrons at favourable prices. Stourbridge retains many buildings of interest despite the fact that many buildings were demolished to accommodate the ring road. The Old Library on the corner of Church Street is now used by the Art College. It was built in 1905 with the aid of £3,000 gift from the philanthropist Andrew Carnegie. It too is decorated with terracotta and has some fine stained glass, very typical of the Victorian era. Barclay's Bank now has a modern frontage at ground floor level but the building itself dates back to the 18th century and has a series of attractive first and second floor windows overlooking the High Street.

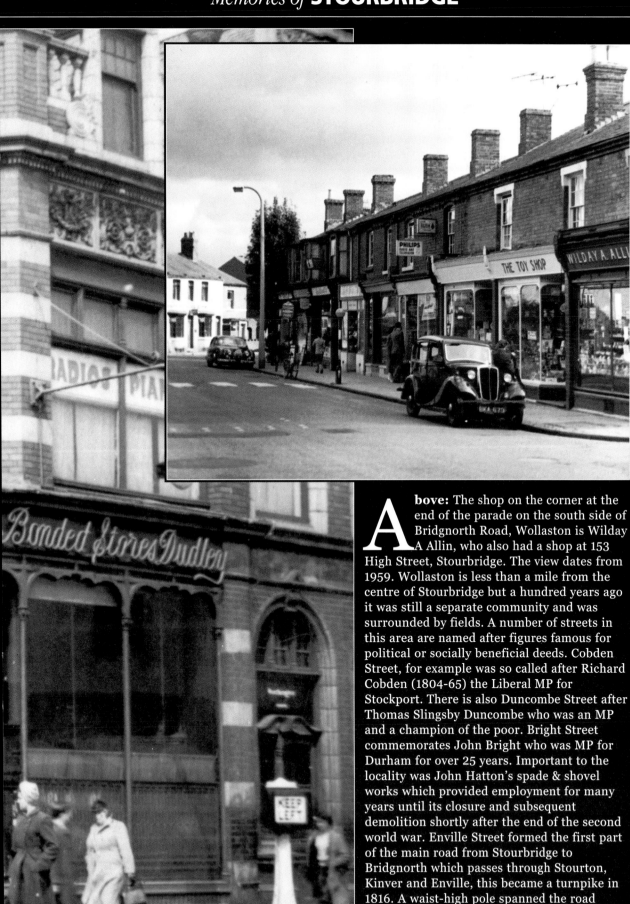

Above: The shop on the corner at the end of the parade on the south side of Bridgnorth Road, Wollaston is Wilday A Allin, who also had a shop at 153 High Street, Stourbridge. The view dates from 1959. Wollaston is less than a mile from the centre of Stourbridge but a hundred years ago it was still a separate community and was surrounded by fields. A number of streets in this area are named after figures famous for political or socially beneficial deeds. Cobden Street, for example was so called after Richard Cobden (1804-65) the Liberal MP for Stockport. There is also Duncombe Street after Thomas Slingsby Duncombe who was an MP and a champion of the poor. Bright Street commemorates John Bright who was MP for Durham for over 25 years. Important to the locality was John Hatton's spade & shovel works which provided employment for many years until its closure and subsequent demolition shortly after the end of the second world war. Enville Street formed the first part of the main road from Stourbridge to Bridgnorth which passes through Stourton, Kinver and Enville, this became a turnpike in 1816. A waist-high pole spanned the road outside the tollkeeper's cottage - the pole was turned once the toll had been paid.

A picture of High Street, Stourbridge as it looked in 1930. On the extreme right you can see the old circulating library. There is a long tradition of reading in the town. There was a reading society it is thought in th early part of the eighteenth century and its members were active in promoting a public subscription library in 1790. The inaugural meeting included Robert Foley (Rector of Oldswinford), John Pattinson (minister at St Thomas's church) James Scott (Presbyterian Minister), William Scott (Author of 'Stourbridge and its vicinity') and Samuel Parkes (Chemist and Author). The subscription was one guinea per annum and for many years this library flourished and periodically issued a printed catalogue of its holdings. It

became known as the Town Library continued to function until the library at the Mechanics' Institute was established when its stock was moved there. It was the generosity of Andrew Carnegie which made the public library a reality. He donated £3,700 towards the project. It started life at the technical School Building, the Reading Rooms and News Rooms opened in August 1905 and the Lending and reference libraries the following year, The clock tower which was built by public subscription in memory of Isaac Nash who had done much to promote the idea of a public library in the town. Over time the library building became unsuitable and it is now housed in the Crown Centre Shopping Centre complex and offers much more than books alone.

Above: The ladies standing in front of the fabric stall in the Market Hall are obviously having an enjoyable time catching up with each other's news, the lady on the left is the stall holder and is passing the time of day until some actual customers turn up. The photographer is standing on the south side of the Market Hall looking towards New Street. The date is December 1958 and by twenty-first century standards there are very few people out doing their Christmas shopping - but then there certainly wasn't the amount of money

around that there is today. The stall on the left in the foreground is Sowerbys of New Street bargain shoe stall. The Crown Shopping Centre and the new Library and Town Council offices now occupy the site of the old Market Hall. The Hall had served the residents of Stourbridge well but this manner of trading became less popular as the twentieth century progressed and the trend for indoor shopping arcades altered to the type found in the Crown Centre and Ryemarket. In effect however, what is most appealing about both the old and the new arrangements is the ability to shop indoors away from traffic and out of the inclement weather. An impassioned appeal by the residents and conservationists of Stourbridge saved the facade of the Market Hall from planned demolition.

Above right: This picture of the War Memorial in High Street, Stourbridge was taken in 1956. The A451 to Kidderminster bends round to the left and the Liverpool, Victoria Insurance offices provide the focal point. The shop on the left of this is Thompsons which advertised itself as 'Housewives' Corner'. An advert in the 'County Express' in July of that year proclaimed, 'Thompsons for quality fresh fruit and veg - for best quality fresh fruit and veg at prices to suit to suit all pockets, shop at Thompsons'. The War Memorial commemorating those who had served in the Royal Worcestershire Regiment, is seen here in its original place in front of the old Free Library before it was transferred to Mary Stevens Park to make room for the inner ring road. The overall design of the memorial was entrusted to Ernest W Pickford who was employed by the Bromsgrove Guild, a reputed firm of art metalworkers. However, the modelling of the symbolic female figure at the top was undertaken by John Cassidy, a well known Manchester sculptor. The memorial was unveiled on 25 February, 1923.

We are looking at the north side of the High Street, Lye from a point near Jackson Street in 1966. Lye was once known as 'the bucket capital of the world' in the days before plastic was heard of. In the seventeenth century local men were employed to extract the plentiful clay and coal deposits of the area. There was also enough iron to be had to make the production of hand made nails possible, and when the manufacture of nails became more a mechanised process in the 1830s the local industry diversified into making buckets, bath, dustbins and trunks, in fact all the 'holloware' for which the district is so well-known. In 1863, George Hill invented the galvanisation process which gave a protective coating to iron by dipping products in a bath of molten zinc. Christ church, Lye was founded in 1813 and became the parish church in 1843. It was built of clay found on the actual site which the men dug and the women moulded into bricks. In 1863 William Booth held a mission in the Primitive Methodist Chapel,Lye, just two years before he was to found the Salvation Army. lye's first public library came in 1922 and was housed in the Council Chamber. It opened two evenings per week. It was demolished in 1933 and the new library now stands on the same site. The district has always boasted numerous pubs - it also had its own Temperance House at one time, this was converted in 1910 to a 460 seat cinema.

Making a living

Supply of gas to Stourbridge, established in 1835 by a limited liability company of six shareholders, actually came from Amblecote which lay just outside the borough at the time. This picture of Stourbridge Gas Works was taken in 1967 shortly before they were demolished. Responsibility for supply was taken over by West Midlands Gas Board under the provisions of the Gas Act, 1948. Holy Trinity Church may be seen in the top centre of the picture with its graveyard adjoining the gas works. Opposite this on the other side of the A491 Wolverhampton to Bromsgrove Road the Holloway End cricket ground may be seen. The railway line which went right into the gas works to provide easy access to coal supplies. This was part of the Great Western Railway line which past through Stourbridge Town station. The Town Station opened in 1879 and offered easier access from the town centre than the Stourbridge Junction Station at Oldswinford which had been operational for four years before this. Coal had originally been transported to the site by canal which is also nearby. The approaches to both Stourbridge stations is via steep gradients necessitating low speeds, but in spite of all precautions there have been one or two hair-raising accidents involving runaway trains. In 1905 a train caused a large amount of damage when it crashed through the goods yard and made a large hole in the wall of the goods office.

Below centre: Once upon a time all milk was sold in glass bottles. This photo taken in Stambermill in 1964 and shows what must have been one of the last milkmen in the country to go on his rounds with a horse drawn float. The motor vehicle has changed the pace of our lives perhaps more than any other invention in the twentieth century. It has altered the distances possible for the journeys to and from work. A hundred years ago a working man could undertake no more than a four or five mile journey as that was the furthest he could walk in an hour or so. Now journeys many times that length are possible in the same time. The car has transformed the way we shop as well. Shopping used to be a daily activity as you were limited to what you could carry in your two hands, but now greater volumes of goods can be transported at a time and weekly and even monthly 'big shops' are commonplace. This has led to the demise of businesses like the one own by the man pictured here and the development of enormous superstores on out of town sites. Which is all very well if you have a car .... Ironically the supermarkets are themselves entering the world of doorstep deliveries

and are offering an ordering service via the internet and so many items are available by mail and electronic mail that in fact now there is no need to go to the shops at all.

Bottom: Dennis Kitson is seen here doing his rounds with his horse and cart at Cross Walks, Lye in July 1958. Kitson's bakery was an essential part of life in Lye and many regretted the loss of fresh bread delivered to the door. The lettering on the canopy on the cart informs us that the bakery baked at least some of its selection of breads from Allinson's flour. It is obviously near the start of the round as there is a large selection of loaves in the cart. Many people who grew up during the heyday of the local baker bemoan the lack of taste in the mass volume bread produced by the big bakeries. Today there is still a vital role for the small baker and supermarkets have recognised the value of freshly baked bread - the selection of breads on offer today, from traditional farmhouse loaves , through French baguettes, focaccia to pittas would have astonished Dennis Kitson's customers, however. There is a striking absence of other traffic on this street, as well as of litter.

It is August, 1955 and the High Street, Stourbridge is undergoing a major reconstruction programme and causing major disruption to normal trading activities. Perhaps the shopkeeper of Hulme's tobacconists is wondering where all his customers have gone. The High Street is still the major shopping street in the town and offers a wide variety of goods in its numerous outlets. It leads to the focal point of the town - the Town Clock. The clock was constructed at the Stourbridge Ironworks of J Bradley & Co in 1857. The mechanism for the clock was originally inside the Market Hall building with drive shafts extending outside to the clock face. For many years the clock was wound under contract by a local firm of jewellers and clockmakers who twice a week had to climb into the loft of Market Hall. Later men from the Stourbridge Council depot in Birmingham Street took on the task. The clock motor was electrified in 1972. In 1989 the clock was removed from its site outside the former entrance to the Market Hall and was taken to be restored. After restoration there was some debate as to where in the town it should stand in the future. However it was restored to its original site in April 1991.

Below centre: It is 16 June, 1963 and a civil defence exercise is being carried out at the Gas Works. The uniform worn by the firemen here served them well for many years but that helmet and indeed the whole outfit somehow seems very cumbersome. The Stourbridge Gas Works was established at Amblecote in 1835 by a limited liability company with six share holders. It was incorporated as a statutory company by the Stourbridge Gas Act of 1855. Gas production was taken over by the West Midlands Gas Board in 1948, but since then gas has ceased to be produced at the plant. As for fire-fighting, this was originally provided by insurance companies but the way they went about things did not please many so in 1879 Henry Turney established a volunteer fire brigade. In the following year a steam fire engine was bought and housed in a fire station in Market Street. When the Town Hall was built it was felt desirable to have a new Fire Station accommodated in that complex. This served the town well until the station in Smithfield was opened in 1926. The service was maintained by public subscription until the coming of

the second world war when it was nationalised. From 1948 the responsibility was transferred to Worcester County Council. A new fire station with training facilities and living accommodation was built in Parkfield - this was opened in September 1968.

Bottom: The telephone was brought to Lye and Stourbridge by the National telephone Co. This photograph shows operators working the old system at the Lye telephone exchange in 1957. Working with all those wires and connections required quick-wittedness and manual dexterity and it seems almost unbelievably complex to those unfamiliar with the set-up. Now so much of what these girls were trained to do is performed by electronic circuits, but many remember fondly the days when you could be sure to speak to a real person at the other end of the phone, nowadays phone conversations are often conducted with pre-recorded messages which tell you to, 'press the star button on your telephone pad' and such like.

A happy band of (mainly women) workers is gathered in the Taylor Law works canteen for a Good Friday service in April, 1957. Judging by their dress there is a mixture of office workers and those involved in actual production - or perhaps the ladies in the full aprons were kitchen staff. They were all contributing in their own way to the manufacture of 'Tala' kitchenware, which included cake tins, bread bins, vegetable racks, tea and sugar canisters, kitchen utensils and the like. There was something of a quiet revolution going on in kitchens up and down the land, new products were on the market, like for example 'Brown & Polson's Flavoured Cornflour' - this 'richest and fruitiest flavour blanc-mange' was offered to the housewife in three flavour packs for eight pence ha'penny or five flavour packs for 1 shilling 3 ha'pence. Also many housewives were choosing to cook with electricity, an advert for Midlands Electricity from the time goes like this: 'that's quick - in seconds they're sizzling, in 10-15 minutes they're cooked to a turn; that's cheap - it costs only a ha'penny to grill chops for all the family - that's electric cooking'.

A "CHAIR" OF STUART CRYSTAL CRAFTSMEN AT WORK

THE FURNACES CONTAIN CRUCIBLES HOLDING HALF A TON OF MOLTEN STUART CRYSTAL.	THE TEAM OR "CHAIR" OF GLASSMAKERS GATHER OUT THE MOLTEN STUART CRYSTAL ON STEEL PIPES AND BLOW AND MANIPULATE IT WHILST IT IS HOT AND PLASTIC.	THE FINISHED ARTICLES OF STUART CRYSTAL ARE PLACED IN THE COOLING FURNACE OR LEHR TO ANNEAL.

Left: A model of a glass-making workshop, illustrating the different processes involved in the production of the highly prized items made in Stuart Crystal and other famous glass producers in the Stourbridge area. The team is called a 'chair' and the label on the model states, ' The furnaces contain crucibles holding half a tone of Stuart Crystal. The team or 'chair' of glassmakers gather out the molten Stuart Crystal on steel pipes and blow and manipulate it whilst it is hot and plastic. The finished articles ... are placed in the cooling furnace or lehr to anneal.' The glass industry has provided employment for thousands over the years and its reputation is truly of international stature. There are no less than three museums exhibiting specimens of the craft from the industry's history including the Broadfield House Museum which exhibits specimens of the craft from the industry's history. Courses on all aspects of glassmaking are still offered to local folk at the International Glass Centre based at Dudley College of Technology. The Glass Department which taught the craft at Stourbridge College has been transferred to Wolverhampton University.

Above: Three people at work in the Webb Corbett stockroom in 1956. They have a pleasant environment in which to work and probably worked no more than forty hours per week. This had not always been the case however. In the mid 1800s men employed in glass manufacture worked about 50 hours per week. They had a shift system in which they worked for six hours and then rest for six hours. There was a quota of work to be accomplished during that time and if the team managed to complete more there was additional pay to be had. Glass-making was also very dangerous. The raw materials, like lead often caused illness, but there were other hazards for those whose job it was to remove pots from the furnaces. A 19th century account of this task noted, that the men were often exhausted with the work and often suffered falls, burns or bruises. One of the most dangerous places to work was in the mixing room where red lead was used. Workers frequently fell ill and died due to the toxicity . Those in the cutting shops also exposed themselves to high risks of inhaling the fine powder used in the polishing process. Boys, sometimes as young as eight were also employed in the glass factory. Their life was very hard as they were fined for the smallest error.

These two women are working at the Yardley & Co Spade and Shovel Works in Stambermill in 1956. They are pressing fork handles. The results of their work are lying on the floor and some specimens are on view hanging above the workbench of the lady on the left. The Town Guide for 1971 lists a number of companies involved in the manufacture of forged and cast products. This industry has been associated with the area since the 17th century aided by the inventiveness of Dud Dudley and Richard Foley. Their ironworks prospered and large factories were built in Stourbridge and Amblecote. Richard Foley was born son of a Dudley nail manufacturer in 1580 and started to manufacture iron in 1620s. He moved to Stourbridge around 1630 and lived at the 'brick-house' in the High Street, a place known to 21st century residents of the town as the Talbot Hotel. By 1636 he was operating five furnaces and nine forges and slitting mills in the West Midlands. He was accused by the Crown of felling 19,320 trees which had been designated for shipbuilding and of having burned annually 300,000 loads of wood in his ironworks over a seven year period. During the Civil War he cast cannon for the king and Prince Rupert stayed with him for three days in October, 1642. Over the years the once large number of small forges declined but their place was taken by firms manufacturing galvanised and enamelled hollow-ware and heating apparatus as well as those making spades, forks and other tools like the one in our picture.

Below centre: It is September 1963 and the new telephone coin boxes are on display at Stourbridge Post Office. This was the beginning of Subscriber Trunk Dialling which was revolutionary at the time of its introduction. Until then all long distance calls had been connected by the operator and seemed to be a major event. Since the arrival of STD as it was commonly known anyone with a telephone could dial their own calls whether they were local or for further afield. It meant there was a new way of writing your telephone number. Previously numbers had been written Stourbridge 1234 now the correct way was Stourbridge (STD 0384) 1234. The display informs us that for 2d you could talk for 10 seconds during the day and for 15 seconds at the cheap rate, after 6pm and at weekends. 1963 was an eventful one on the wider stage, the assassination of President John F Kennedy took place that year, as did the Great Train Robbery, when over £1 million was stolen from a Post Office mobile railway carriage after the train stopped at a

bogus red signal. It was also the year that Lord Beeching announced a swingeing series of cuts in the routes, schedules and staff of British Rail. On a lighter note four lads calling themselves The Beatles were causing a stir throughout the world.

Top: There is a cheerful atmosphere in this workroom at Mark Palfrey & Co in 1956, a company which had at the time over a hundred years of experience in the leather tanning trade. The two ladies in the foreground are busy stitching using their Singer sewing machines. It is quite likely they also had a domestic Singer model at home as these machines were in mass production and proving very popular, enabling clothes and soft furnishings to be 'run up' at home, saving a small fortune in the process. The dressing of leather, including the production of sheepskin rugs and the manufacture of chamois leather played an important role in the local economy of Stourbridge.

A legacy of learning

Old Swinford Hospital is a school famous not just in Strourbridge but well known throughout Britain.

The school was founded in 1667, receiving its first eight pupils in 1670 when the 'Founder's building was completed.

The Founder in question was Thomas Foley, a Great Witley man who had made a fortune manufacturing iron goods, earning a then huge income of £5,000 a year. A local preacher persuaded him to found a school for poor boys. On his death in 1677 Foley left the the school the whole manor of Pedmore, the adjacent parish, and lands and property in Warwickshire, Staffordshire, Oldswinford and Dudley. Foley also left £2,000 to be invested in land which was bought at Rowley Regis and Stone in Staffordshire.

The rent received from the lands was more than sufficient for the expenses of the school right up to the end of the second world war; until then every boy who attended was educated free of charge, as a boarder.

Thomas Foley decided that his school should be for 60 boys from 'poor but honest homes' and that the entry age should be between the ages of 7 and 11. The syllabus, laid down by Foley, stated that the pupils should be taught their catechism, to read, to write and the 'cast accounts'.

The chosen boys were nominated by 18 Feoffees, or trustees, whose successors still administer the estates and income - with males of the Foley family having the right to three places. The remaining lands now amount to some 600 acres around Stourbridge including the Stourbridge Golf Course. Much of the income is used

Top left: Thomas Foley. **Above:** *An early line drawing of the school.* **Below:** *A typical class c1887.*

school was often referred to as the Blue Coat School, and still is by older inhabitants of Stourbridge, a very few of whom may still remember the boys marching to church in uniform on Sunday mornings up until 1929.

Few schools are called 'hospital'. The word is derived from the Latin 'Hospes' - a guest - which also gave us the words host and hospitality. The word hospital was once used to encompass the care of many different groups not just the sick but also school children and the aged poor.

Income of the Old Swinford Hospital increased during the 18th century and as a result in 1830 the Feoffees increased the number of boys to 70 although the Charity Commissioners, noting the level of income to be £2,400 in 1832, felt that even more could be done. The Commissioners recommended that numbers

to help parents on low income pay boarding costs and some to provide additional amenities at the school.

The original school uniform, the Blue Coat uniform of the 17th century apprentice, was retained until 1928. The first modification came however in 1836 when corduroy trousers replaced blue cloth breeches. In the early days boys also wore blue stockings and linen bands to stiffen their collars. In the 19th century a boy was given two suits of clothing on entering the school and one suit, three shirts, four pairs of stockings, three pairs of shoes and a cap each year. On leaving school, when he was finally apprenticed, he was given two suits of clothes. As a result of the pupils' uniform the

Above left: *The school about 1910.*
Top: *Old Swinford Hospital Parade at the end of the 19th century.* **Right:** *An 1920s view of the school.*

should be increased and that better facilities, especially for fresh air and exercise, could be provided.

As a result of the Charity Commissioners report, the number of pupils was further increased, first to 80, and shortly thereafter to 100. A barn behind the school, now known as the Barn Block, was converted and extended to provide a dormitory and school room for fifty boys. Diet, school hours, uniform and play facilities were all reviewed and new regulations agreed. The diet was certainly not terribly appetising in those days with bread and milk being prescribed for breakfast and supper every day, and bread and cheese for lunch three days each week.

Boys rose at 6.00 am in summer and 6.30 in winter and went to bed at 8.00 pm, attending prayers twice a day at 9.00am and 6.00pm. Holidays were a month at Christmas and five weeks in the summer. The total hours spent at lessons each week however, were 30, only a little more than today.

After 1835 the boys were divided into four classes of 25 boys each. The boys were taught only by a headmaster and an undermaster who used senior boys to assist them. The curriculum was updated around this time to include geography and history in addition to the three Rs and Bible reading. By 1846 the Feoffees described the school as a surprisingly modern sounding 'commercial school'. Later, from 1848, some boys would also attend drawing and modelling classes at the Art School in Stourbridge.

The increasing emphasis on academic competence had been underlined in 1836 when exams were introduced twice each year, with a Christmas leaving exam for

Below: *Sports day in the 1950s.* **Above:** *A school group in the 1930s.*

school was in a state of rebellion. The ring leader, a boy named Davies, was expelled. As a result of the troubles the Feoffees decreed that any boy who ran away was to be brought back and well flogged by the headmaster in the presence of the whole school; a second offence meant expulsion.

Expulsion was by no means uncommon. And such a sanction was not always without good reason: in 1704 no fewer than 12 boys were expelled for beating and abusing their Master and it took some time to fill the places.

Despite the occasional expulsion the pupil roll increased to 120 in 1862 and to 160 in 1883 when the boarding house now called Maybury was built. A few years earlier a sanatorium, now Foster House, had been built. By the 1920s however as a result of a decline in both finances and the demand for apprentices numbers fell back to 125.

In 1928 the new headmaster, Mr Stone, introduced a number of reforms including a change of uniform to a less archaic style of dress. And rugby was introduced. Despite changes, however, numbers continued to fall with barely 100 pupils enrolled by the outbreak of the second world war.

During the war numbers fell even further until by 1945 there were only 70 boys in the school. Financial difficulties continued and the school began to look for other sources of income. In September 1946 10 boys

those due to be apprenticed. The Feoffees gave prizes to the most successful.

But along with the carrot went the stick. Discipline in the Victorian era was strict, though perhaps not as strict as earlier times: in the 17th century there had been stocks set up in the school courtyard! The punishment book from the period 1838 to 1913 has survived and records many canings and floggings. Demotion could also be a punishment; a 'Sergeant' or 'prefect' might be demoted to 'Corporal' or a 'Corporal' be demoted to the ranks.

The most frequent offence was 'running away'. On 21st September 1854 no fewer than 44 boys ran away, nearly half the school, in a mass break out. The following year the headmaster reported that the whole

Top: Prize giving in the 1920s. **Above:** *Boys studying in the library in the 1960s.* **Right:** *Cadets on exercise.*

entered the school as boarders paid for by Worcester County Council because of their home circumstances. Soon other boys followed, sent by local authorities in London and the Midlands - and from even further afield. By 1947 there were only 42 pupils being paid for by the Feoffees but 34 by Local Authorities. The next year the first fee paying pupils were also received with total numbers rising to 98 pupils of whom only 27 were boys paid for by the Feoffees.

The whole basis of funding therefore began quickly to change and in 1949 Voluntary Aided status was granted. All the educational side of the school's expenses was met by Worcestershire County Council whilst boarding costs were met by the Feoffees, Local Authorities or parents. It might have been possible for the school to become a successful independent boarding school at this time, but to do so only boys from affluent backgrounds would have been able to attend, contrary to what the Founder had intended.

Modest progress was soon being made with a small sixth form being established in 1951 with the first A levels taken in 1953.

The school became officially classified as a grammar/technical school which brought in a more academic type of boy. A number of free places were provided for local day boys as the price of obtaining Voluntary Aided status; this proved advantageous when the number of boarders began to decline after peaking at 250 in the early 1970s.

Following local government reorganisation in 1974 Stourbridge found itself no longer in Worcestershire but in Dudley with new educational policies. Old Swinford took its first comprehensive pupils in 1976 from Dudley, though its grammar school tradition ensured that its GCSE and A Level results were far ahead of national averages; sixth formers have achieved over 90 per cent pass rates at A level since 1990.

The change to Dudley stopped the flow of pupils from Worcestershire's feeder schools. By 1978 the number of boarders had fallen to 150 with a sixth form of fewer than 50. Day boys comprised more than half the total in a school of just over 300 pupils.

In 1979 the Feoffees and Governors, with the support of the Local Authority, decided on a radical policy of actually expanding boarding provision, with a parallel commitment to raise pupil numbers to 500. This was achieved by dramatically increasing the number of boys for whom parents paid full boarding costs. The number and quality of boys entering at 13 from independent preparatory schools also rose rapidly throughout the 1980s. In order to attract academically able boys the Feoffees provide money for scholarships, initially for boys at 13, but also more recently for 11 year olds and sixth formers.

Top left: *Science class, 1979.* ***Top right:*** *A 1980s aerial view of the school.* ***Left:*** *The Head with the senior boys in the 1960s.*

During the 1980s as four new boarding houses and other facilities were built for the extra boarders, the school became ever more successful both academically and on the sports field. As a result more and more boys and their parents began to press for places in the school from all over the country and applications began to greatly exceed the available places. To enable the Feoffees to put up all the new buildings the Department of Education and Science via the Dudley Local Education Authority made a considerable financial investment in the school and the Feoffees, whose financial position was stronger than it had been for some time, supported with their own resources the greatest building programme since the school's foundation. The Feoffees contributed 15 per cent of the cost of each new building. The sixth form grew to 180 and all boarders in the sixth form had their own study bedrooms.

In 1989 the school Governors and Feoffees seized the opportunity to become one of the first Grant Maintained schools. The decision to 'go it alone' was approved in the statutory ballot by over 96 per cent of parents.

The move was soon judged beneficial. Applications to the school increased even further and success in and outside of the classroom has never been higher. The school set out to be a market leader in boarding provision for boys from all kinds of backgrounds with the clear goal of university degree courses to follow on from the sixth form, with virtually all sixth formers now applying for such courses. A significant number of boys gain places at Oxford and Cambridge Universities.

Whilst all these changes have occurred, the school is still careful to follow the Founder's intent that boys from less affluent homes should find a place with the support of the financial resources of the Feoffees. An Old Swinford boy learns to mix easily with people from all walks of life, to eschew arrogance, not to take anyone for granted, but to respect everyone for their individual worth. Old Swinford by its long history, traditions and present arrangement is thought by many to be unique among the boarding schools of this country and to be an ideal model for the boarding school of the future.

Building on site continues with an extension to the music centre at Hanbury House completed in 1999 and a magnificent new Sports Centre in 2000. But ultimately it is the quality of the boys, not the structures, which mark the school's real triumph.

Today British families from all over the world send their sons to Old Swinford Hospital, attracted by the school's relatively small size, its excellent facilities, fine standards of care and its outstanding academic results.

Top left: The current Head, Mr Potter with Kenneth Clarke in 1990, opening the new technology block. **Left (top):** *The Quad today.* **Left (bottom):** *Foley House in 1985.*

A healthy set of tubes

A well functioning body needs a good set of tubes. A customer requiring steel conduit, exhaust pipes and galvanised cylindrical products need look no further than the healthy company operating at Balds Lane, Lye. Hayes Tubes Ltd, or Hayes Conduit Co as it was until the 1950s, has been meeting those needs since before the war. However, it is not a company to rest on its laurels. Already an employer of 55 staff it intends to double the size of its business as the 21st century develops.

Part of its optimism is based upon the intelligent use of investment it has made over the years. When new equipment has been bought the company has always gone for new machinery of tried and tested design. In that way it has ensured that it has been tooled up to the best of specifications without taking the chancy step of becoming a guinea pig. Let others do the experimentation and we will reap the rewards has been the sensible approach. Cost effectiveness has been the benefit as productivity rose. A new tube mill and new premises were installed close to the original premises as recently as 2000 to help the expansion.

Hayes Tubes has been at the cutting edge of the tube making industry for many years and the future looks assured. However, the management is not complacent and is always looking to strengthen its position. Quite often it has needed to look no further than itself to do just that, because there is

Left: *Second generation, Oswald Penn.*
Below: *The offices under demolition.*
Bottom: *HF Weld Mill, purchased in 1968.*

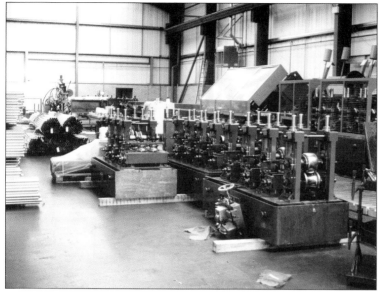

considerable expertise within the company ranks. 'If you want a job doing well, do it yourself' is not always a motto that can be lived up to. The workforce and directors at Hayes Tubes often have. In the 1980s development work at the site was largely carried out by in-house staff. Management worked alongside other employees to erect a new office building. New factory flooring was laid and machinery installed by the very same people. That the bosses took off their jackets and got stuck in went down well. It has been that sort of attitude that has helped a sense of togetherness in the business that cannot be measured, though the result can be observed in the quality of workmanship. IT was officially recognised when the quality control and guarantee code of the British Standard 5750 was awarded in the mid 1980s

The company has a long association with engineering that dates back to the 1860s. However, it is in 1936 that the story of Hayes Tubes Ltd really begins. AC and JS Penn were part of a family concern that owned rolling mills in Cradley Heath and the Stourbridge area. They bought out a tube making factory owned by Jackson and Kendrick. Where welded tubes were to be made there had once

been a company making loudspeakers for the gramophone industry. Nipper, the HMV dog, could well have had his ear to one of the speakers that had been produced at Balds Lane. Before long loudspeakers carried the sound of 'Workers' Playtime' to the shop floor as the machines hummed and furnaces glowed as the welding process went on. The Penn cousins did not run the production side. They handed over the day to day running of the business to the next generation of the family, Oswald Penn. He found a buyer for the stock that was inherited from Jackson and Hendrick and started manufacturing a line of products that has served the automotive and construction industries well ever since. During the war the tube mills played a vital role in contributing to the war effort. Production seemed to be almost non stop, though the provision of raw materials was a continual headache. Many of the workforce, having supported king and country during the day, continued to do so in the evening. They became fire watchers, ambulance drivers and first aiders.

Oswald, for many years, was the company chairman and oversaw the purchase of a new mill in 1969 that helped the firm through a sticky patch. When he retired in 1971 he was quoted as saying that he thought there were still a few years left in the production of conduit, even though others thought it was dying on its feet. Oswald knew what he was talking about as it still has a large part to play in the industry. A third generation of the family, represented by cousins Anthony and Jeremy, took over as joint managing directors until the latter's death in January 2000. Their introduction into the industry could hardly have come at a worse time. The country was bedevilled with industrial unrest. The prime minister, Edward Heath, had introduced the 3 day week. But, the cousins overcame those initial difficulties and helped build Hayes Tubes to its present position of strength.

Left: *The new offices of Hayes Tubes.*
Top left: *The new factory completed in 2000.*
Top right: *Supplier of the Year Award, August 2000.*

Coached to perfection

'Ten green bottles hanging on a wall...' How many of us recall singing that classic song at the top of our young voices on coach trips to the seaside? Come to think of it how many of us still recall coaches being referred to as 'Charas', that now almost forgotten abbreviation of charabanc? Many of our happiest childhood memories stem from daytrips on coaches to who knows where: the journey was as important as the destination with not only community singing but the promise of pop, sandwiches and ice-cream to brighten the day.

One firm which has done more than most to contribute to our memories is Lye-based Prospect Coaches (West) Ltd.

The business dates back to 1956 when Geoff and Ruby Watts purchased an ex pawnbrokers shop, Prospect House, at 112, Cemetery Road, Lye. Together they renovated the shop and reopened it as a general store.

In 1957 Geoff started his first transport company by purchasing a black 'London taxi' which was run from the taxi rank in Stourbridge, the minimum fare then being half a crown (12.5p). Although by now the couple had four children to care for Geoff could not stop at one taxi and before long he had bought minibuses with which he delivered school dinners to local schools.

Seven years later, in 1967, Geoff decided he wanted larger vehicles and bought his first coach, a Seddon, registration number SWB 200. Late in the 1960s the

Left: *Founder, Geoff Watts.*
Below: *Part of the fleet in 1969.*
Bottom: *A picture of Geoff Watts in 1973.*

growing transport company moved to the site of the C&V garage at King Street, Wollaston; the site being purchased from the Don Everall corporation. Double-decker buses were now added to the expanding fleet.

Over the years many other local companies were absorbed including such established names as Deluxe Coaches of Enville Street, Stourbridge, Favourite Coaches and Hayes Coaches both of High Street, Lye. Falcon Garage, the premises of Hayes Coaches, were later acquired and the company still trades from that same address at 81 High Street, today. Further companies were also bought out over the passing years: Bearwood Coaches, Homer Luxury Travel of Quarry Bank, Davenports of Cinderbank Netherton and Parkes of Quarry Bank.

All the companies were purchased along with the licences they held for transporting day trippers and holiday makers to their various holiday destinations - since deregulation such licences are no longer required.

During those years many workers were ferried to and from various sites of BSR at Stourbridge and Old Hill, Austin's at Longbridge, BIP at Oldbury, Birmetals at Woodgate and Ewarts at Dudley. Conductors were required to collect fares from passengers and the 'Setright' ticket system was used.

Throughout that time Prospect grew rapidly and by now three of the Watt's children were working for the firm: Glynne and Lynton, the eldest sons, being employed as drivers later being joined by the Watts' only daughter Roslynd who left the banking industry to join the business in 1974. Later the Watt's youngest son Grenville would also join the family firm as a driver.

Still not satisfied Geoff sought new challenges and bought the businesses of Fred Jones in Aberdare South Wales followed by Ladvale Ltd of Gloucestershire. The latter company causing numerous problems when many undisclosed items came to light.

It was at this time that the firm was remodelled and returned to concentrate on its routes in the Black Country alone. The company was renamed Prospect Coaches West Ltd.

Once again the business has successfully grown, the core of the company now being the provision of transport for local authorities for home to school transport, sports and swimming baths and educational visits. Private hire is also undertaken for many individuals and clubs. Some of the children now carried on the company's coaches have grandparents who travelled with the same firm.

Today only Geoff, Ruby and Roslynd remain in the company: between them they collectively boast more than a century of experience in the coaching industry. With both Geoff and Ruby into their retirement years however may tasks have passed to their daughter. Roslynd continues to ensure that the company remains at its efficient and friendly best with the support of her husband Ian - who is himself the youngest son of yet another local coaching family, Hadley's of Quarry Bank.

Top left: *Geoff and Ruby Watts with their youngest son, Grenville, in 1978.* **Top right:** *A Prospect coach on its way to Blackpool.* **Below:** *One of the coaches today.*

Ruling the world

I s there any reader who did not own a Helix geometry set during their schooldays? Most of us did. Founded in 1887 Helix Ltd is the oldest and largest manufacturer of student drawing instruments in the UK. On its 6.5 acre site in Engine Lane, Lye, it employs more than 200 people.

Helix produces and distributes a vast range of products for schools, offices and the home together with stationery sundries such as erasers, stencils, computer cleaning products, cash boxes and security cabinets.

The firm was founded by Frank Shaw, the son of a Birmingham goldsmith. Frank Shaw began his working life as an engineer making small items from wood and brass. Later he turned his skills to producing high quality laboratory products such as clamps and stands but soon saw a demand for drawing instruments.

Three terraced houses, 51-55 Newhall Hill, Birmingham, were converted into a small factory where Frank Shaw's Universal Woodworking Company began production making amongst other items wooden rulers and set-squares. At the same time Shaw's other company, Hall Street Metal, marketed a range of drawing equipment. The two firms merged in 1892 moving some production to premises at 21 Newhall Hill.

In 1894 Frank Shaw invented the Helix Patent Ring Compass, in which the pencil was held in the compass by a finger-

tightened ring rather than, as in all previous models, by using a screwdriver to tighten a screw.

Australia became the company's first export market in 1898. Sales of 'Helix - the King of Compasses' exceeded all expectations. By the end of the century the company's product range was vast including not only office equipment but even wooden candle-sticks and metal hair curlers.

The first set of mathematical equipment aimed specifically at schoolchildren was marketed in 1912, containing a compass, protractor, six inch ruler, a pencil and a rubber.

Frank Shaw retired in 1919, selling the firm to his solicitor's clerk Arthur Lawson and his works manager Alfred Westwood for £10,000. At the time of

Top left: *Shaw's second compass patent.*
Top right: *A typical drawing class in the 1880s.*
Above centre: *A Helix catalogue from 1966.* **Below left:** *Arthur Lawson.* **Below:** *Gordon Lawson (seated third from left) pictured with the sales team in 1959.*

equipment continued to be made.

Alfred Westwood died in 1941 and Gordon Lawson became general manager. Arthur Lawson died in 1952.

Cliff Westwood retired in 1954 and sold his shareholding to Gordon Lawson, signalling a major change in the business. In 1955 the company name was changed to The Helix Universal company Ltd and production was rapidly increased, including a weekly output of 40,000 wooden rulers! In that same year new factory premises were found at Lye to accommodate the growing firm.

Tragically the energetic Gordon Lawson died suddenly in 1959. His wife Elsie and eldest son Peter however grasped the reins, introducing the first plastic rulers that same year. In 1960 company turnover had been a little over half a million pounds - by 1980 this had risen to £7 million, much of the growth being due to exports - an increase largely due to the efforts of Elsie Lawson who spent several years ceaselessly travelling the globe in search of sales, culminating in her being awarded the OBE in 1966 for her services to exports.

By 1968 when Elsie Lawson retired, the company was the foremost manufacturer of school equipment in the world. Peter Lawson succeeded her as chairman, her role as export manager being taken by her younger son Mark Lawson, who would in due course become chairman of the company himself.

Today the company manufactories 650 different products and sells another 750 under the Helix name, exporting to 85 countries. In the future the firm plans to expand in the USA, where it already has a subsidiary, and Europe and to acquire more manufacturing companies which can be moved to Lye.

the sale the company employed around 70 staff with annual sales of £17,000.

By 1920 sales had risen to £25,000 but remained at that level for many years. The partners' sons, Gordon Lawson and Cliff Westwood, joined the company in 1925.

The years of economic recession soon followed but by 1935 expansion began again starting with the acquisition of 56 and 57 Newhall Hill. Even those premises were soon to prove inadequate and production was moved to Balsall Heath on the eve of the second world war.

During the war production shifted to making metal bound chests for the navy as well as shell plugs and navigators' instruments though some school room

Top left: *The Lye factory today.*
Top right: *Elsie Lawson.*
Above: *Princess Diana's visit to Helix in June 1987 to celebrate the company's centenary.*
Right: *One of Helix's ranges today.*

King of the Hill

How many of us can recall the first television set in our homes? Many readers will still recall what life was like before every house and flat contained a television. Not until the 1960s did the ownership of televisions seriously challenge the radio, or wireless as we all once knew it. And what about all those other goods we now take for granted: washing machines, dishwashers, hi-fi sets and video recorders? Every generation has a clear memory of the first time they saw this or that wonder of the electronic age.

We see electrical goods as perfectly normal these days, but until the late 1950s they were very much luxury goods. Not until the approach of the 1960s did we begin to realise that the things we had only seen in Hollywood films in the affluent USA might be something we too could aspire to. And in truth we really could begin to hope after the seemingly endless austerity years during and after the war. Prime Minister Harold Macmillan rightly said we had never had it so good. Full employment was back for the first time in a generation and new hire purchase schemes meant affordability for all. Those who had the foresight to anticipate what would happen in the sector of the market

selling consumer durables such as electrical goods had the opportunity to ride a wave of commercial success never before experienced in Britain. And one surfer on the commercial seas who managed to catch his wave was Stourbridge's Geoff Hill.

The Geoff Hill Ltd Gas and Electrical Superstore now based in High Street, Amblecote has been around for as long as many youngsters can remember; but who is Geoff Hill? Geoff Hill was born in 1927 at his parent's home in Trinity Street, Brierley Hill. Geoff attended Bent Street infant's school and Brookmoor junior school before obtaining a scholarship to King Edward VI School in Stourbridge in 1938. Geoff however left school at the age of 15 having decided that the academic life was not for him, being far more interested in his passion for cycle racing.

In fact the list of jobs Geoff took during his teens and twenties was quite remarkable; on leaving school he got a job as assistant store keeper at the Prestwood TB Sanatorium; he then went to work as the sole assistant to an aged accountant in Dudley - using the opportunity to develop a facility for figures which would stand him in good stead later in life. Towards the end of the second world war Geoff was called up for national service. As it

Above: *Geoff Hill, the company founder.*
Below: *A night-time view of the original premises in 1958.*

turned out his service would not be in the armed forces but in the coalmines, Geoff becoming one of the 'Bevan boys' and being conscripted to work in coalmining. After surface training Geoff was sent to Hilton Main Colliery and undertook the most arduous work underground - permanent back trouble would be a lasting legacy of his time down the pit. It would put an end to his successful career as a racing cyclist not long after he became the 'National Junior Time Trial Champion'.

Following his period of national service Geoff Hill and his first wife, whom he had married in 1949, took on a grocery shop on the riverside at Bewdley, before taking over the Hop Pole Inn where they stayed for the next three years. During the week when things were quiet Geoff began a remarkable business in 'Pixies'; he found a producer in Birmingham, arranged for hand painting by out workers in the district and, after also sourcing other suitable goods drove them down to retail outlets in Somerset and Devon. Before founding his own business Geoff also sold typewriters for Glovers in Wolverhampton and also took up a similar position for Bakers of Walsall. It was however five years spent as a representative for the Hoover Company, which gave Geoff a feel for electrical goods and an awareness of their enormous sales potential.

In 1958 the now famous Geoff Hill business began at 118 Brettell Lane, Amblecote, a small two-room shop, which he rented for £3 per week. An astute business man even then he quite soon sub-let the upstairs to the Provident Clothing Company for £3 per week too! Before long the large grocers shop next door run by George Mason, then a well-known chain, became vacant so Geoff took that over, really extending his operation and staying for the next 22 years.

In the early years electrical items like washing machines and vacuum cleaners not only had to be sold but also delivered and demonstrated. Every Monday morning (because everyone washed on Monday mornings in those days) Geoff was out first thing delivering a washing machine, filling it up with hot water, doing the first wash, showing the customer how to power ring the clothes or spin dry them, dependant on which type of machine he was demonstrating. He then went quickly back to the shop to repeat the process for two or three customers! The Brettell Lane shop was a success from the outset; times were perfect with ever increasing growth in demand for electrical consumer goods. Turnover increased each year with Geoff winning manufacturer's prizes for sales every year, including a memorable trip to Bermuda as well as cruises.

Geoff's pleasant and helpful manner with customers, as well as his own self financing hire purchase scheme introduced after a disagreement with a finance company, led to him building up a tremendous reputation locally for fair trading.

Top: *The original premises with delivery van, parked at the roadside, ready to deliver that new appliance to a waiting customer.*
Above centre: *Geoff cycling in his hey-day.*

Progress was helped immeasurably by participating in a 'national buying group' made up of 850 independent retailers, giving members the purchasing power of much larger businesses. Geoff became a director of the group and his store became one of the top ten independent electrical stores in the whole country. So successful did the business become that by the late 1970s even larger premises would have to be found. In November 1981 the business moved just around the corner to the present Superstore in Amblecote High Street, a former car showroom.

Best Price, Best Choice, Best Service has been the firm's slogan over the years and they have always tried their hardest to live up to it. Sometimes customers bought items in the shop and the goods were delivered so quickly to their homes that in some cases the van was waiting before they arrived back home!

For the past ten years Geoff's younger brother, Robert, has been Managing Director, carrying on running the business with the attention to detail and good service shown by Geoff over the years. The highly motivated staff who regularly undertake product knowledge training on all the diverse range of appliances on show, are now all share holders in the company. Geoff's personal motto throughout his business life is "you are only as good as the weakest member of your staff". He, and now brother Robert, have always been proud of the loyal band of dedicated workers who have contributed so highly to the reputation the store has had throughout the region for all these years.

Celebrating 30 years in business in 1998, Geoff gave away 30 television sets to local charities. Ten years later 40 TVs were given away to celebrate 40 years in business. Charity has been very much at the centre of Geoff Hill's life. On taking semi-retirement, although retaining chairmanship of the company, Geoff set up a Charitable Trust and donated 10 per cent of his

Above: *Appearing in "Love on the dole", Geoff Hill, standing right, with other members of the cast of the Dudley Little Theatre Company, with whom Geoff performed in the late 1940s.*
Below: *The premises in the 1980s.*

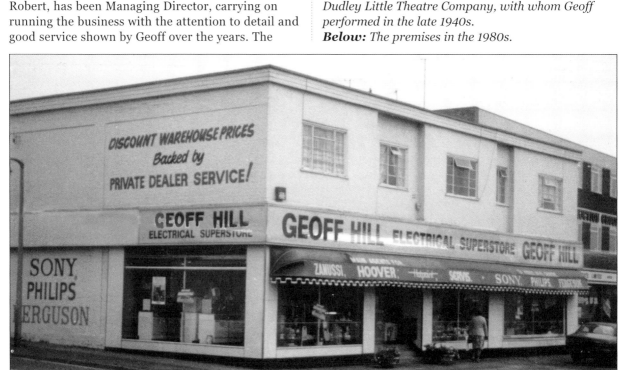

Hospice", opening hospice shops throughout the black country, Stourbridge, Brierley Hill, Cradley Heath, Dudley, Lower Gornal and Halesowen. Under Geoff's leadership the hospice trading company has raised in excess of £1 million.

In 1996 a hospice lottery was started which Geoff promoted which now raises several thousand pounds each week. Such enthusiasm is all the more poignant when one learns that around the

shares in the company to it. In effect 10 per cent of the firm's profits now go to the Charitable Trust and are used to help charities and needy causes throughout the district. Such a gesture has been far from untypical: Geoff Hill has supported local charities for decades, for example making an early effort to raise money to buy a mini-bus for the residential home where his handicapped daughter lives - a gesture repeated when the first mini-bus reached it's "sell buy date".

Yet another interest of Geoff's is the "Hope Trust" established to provide money to give Christmas presents to under-privileged children in the borough of Dudley. Geoff has also enthusiastically supported the hospice movement, becoming a leading fundraiser and also chairman of a Trading Company established to raise funds for "Mary Stevens

time the super store opened Geoff himself was found to have a cancerous condition three months after his marriage to his second wife, Sue. Fortunately after months of hospital treatment the condition was cured. Before the end of the millennium Geoff would look to the future of marketing and start up another company, this time based in London. The new company, run by Geoff's stepson Richard, now sells gas and electrical appliances over the Internet. Geoff Hill has marked the changes from black and white television to the age of satellites, CDs and computers; what will readers 50 years from now make of today's electrical goods, one wonders?

Top: *Geoff Hill and his dedicated staff ready to give service with a smile.* ***Above:*** *The current premises.*

Learning all day and every day

When the Labour government swept to power in 1997 it did so partly on the education ticket. The new prime minister, Tony Blair, had vowed to make 'education, education, education' a major thrust of his party's input. For many this was nothing new. People involved in child care and development had been focusing on this long before the politicians decided to flag it up as a vote winner. Teachers and workers at Clent's Sunfield School had been dedicating themselves to the interests of youngsters since the

1930s. Set in 58 acres of delightful woodland and open pasture, the school today caters for the needs of up to 85 children aged from 6 to 19 who have severe or complex learning needs. There is also

Left: Founders Friedrich Geuter and Michael Wilson.
Below: Bedtime at Sunfield in the 1960s.
Bottom: Main House, c1960.

requirements, but still retains Steiner's basic belief in the value of each individual, whatever his circumstances. The school was originally located in a small house in Selly Oak, Birmingham.

The first carers were a small band of young men and women who had given up their own jobs to devote themselves to what they saw as a worthwhile and charitable exercise.

specialist provision for children with autism and challenging behaviour. Sunfield is in operation around the clock, 365 days each year and the young people who attend the school do so on a residential basis. Family circumstances or the nature of their children's disabilities have meant that the provision at home or in mainstream education is inappropriate. It takes considerable numbers and a high level of expertise to attend to the demands of those resident at the school and Sunfield currently employs over 300 dedicated staff.

Sunfield was established in 1930 by a professional musician, Michael Wilson, and Dr Friedrich Geuter. Originally, Wilson and Geuter were inspired by the work and beliefs of Rudolf Steiner. The modern Sunfield has taken the school's approach along more practical paths these days in line with Ofsted and Social Services

Sunfield

It was a struggle in those early days as public perception of disability was so different from the view taken today. Now we rejoice in the success of our athletes taking part in the Paralympics. In the 1930s we turned our gaze away. Out of sight, out of mind was the order of the day.

Although the initial financial outlook was bleak as the number of residents grew, donations and loans enabled the dedicated directors and staff to purchase Clent Grove, the house and grounds that now form the heart of the modern school. Dr Geuter, Michael Wilson and the staff knew that self help was the best that could be achieved. Even a large part of the school's furniture was made in the workshops on site. In those initial difficult times money was so tight that anyone needing something as straightforward as a new pair of shoes had to go cap in

Top left and right: *Classes in the 1960s.*
Above centre: *A brochure from the 1960s.*

hand to the financial director for an allowance. The usual answer was, 'We will see what we can do at the end of the month.'

The community spirit of all who worked there during this era paid off tremendously. Without their willingness to pull together and share tasks it is doubtful that the school could have survived, less still have developed into a major force in the education of the disabled.

Gradually things improved. Continuity helped the situation even further. Dr Geuter's son became involved and Michael Wilson was still a director some 40 years after Sunfield took in its first resident. The school had become recognised as one of the leaders in its educational sector. This was recognised nationally when Michael Wilson was the subject of a 'This is Your Life' TV programme in the 1960s. By then Sunfield had also seen many additional buildings appear at Clent Grove. Therapy through play, painting, music and movement was promoted and a small farming project encouraged children to be involved in the growing of produce and animal husbandry. By 1968 there were six special classes, a new hall had been built to complement the various workshops and one particularly notable venture was the specially

designed pool. This was used for hydro and colour therapy. Michael Wilson conducted a lot of research into this latter approach and some of his work continues today.

In more recent years Sunfield seemed to lose its way, falling behind the educational times. Following the 1996 inspection by Ofsted, the government's educational watchdog, Sunfield was placed under 'special measures'. This prompted the appointment of a new chief executive and principal,

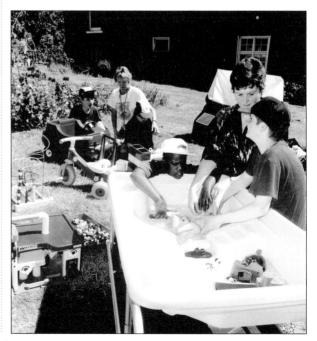

Top: *Jasper Carrott with Martin Coyne of Peopleton & Appleby (Birmingham). present a Variety Club Sunshine Coach to Sunfield in March 2000.* **Right:** *Outdoor play for one of the children's houses in the 1990s.*

local authorities, but the school also relies on donations for all its capital development and purchases ie. building work, vehicles and equipment. There are now 12 residential houses on site in addition to the classrooms, halls, theatre, gym, library, sensory rooms and kitchens. Children are not hidden away as once might have been the approach in the early years of the last century.

Professor Barry Carpenter, the following year to help draft and enact a development plan to turn the school round. The accommodation and facilities were upgraded, new staff recruited and new policies and procedures established. A further Ofsted inspection in July 1998took Sunfield out of special measures and showed that Sunfield had not just turned the corner. It was off and running down the street once more. At a London Conference in 1999 David Blunkett, Secretary of State for Education was moved to say that the challenge of improvement had been met admirably and Sunfield was marked out as being one of the most improved schools in the country. The Social Services Inspectorate mirrored the praise in its report of December 1998 and Sunfield gained an Investors in People award the following year.

Today children come to Sunfield from all over the country. It is an independent residential school registered with the DFEE and a registered charity. The care and education costs are usually paid by

They use community facilities such as swimming baths, leisure centres and local clubs, and go out to the cinema, play ten-pin bowling and attend scout and guide groups. Every child has his own individual education and care plan. There is a wide variety of abilities reflected in the school population and the curriculum is designed to reflect this. There is a balance between the National Curriculum and the school's own integrated learning curriculum. Children respond to the targets set for them which are both achievable and demanding. The attitude of management , teaching and care staff is vital in the students' development. Adult expectation counts for so much. Here, at Sunfield, they seem to have got it right. Focus is placed upon what can be done, not upon what the limitations are. As the old song says, 'Accentuate the positive'.

Parents are also encouraged to play as involved a role as they can and Sunfield offers a range of family services as well as having a dedicated family liaison worker and family centre. Sunfield opens its doors on a regular basis to other local schools and community groups. The conference centre hosts courses and workshops for educators and people from other professions. The school hopes to provide a further family centre, school buildings and houses over the next 10 years but whatever the bricks and mortar, Sunfield will continue to provide a student orientated education within its specialist approach as it gives each one the opportunity to achieve his potential as a valuable member of society.

Top left: *Sunfield hosted the Clent children's Millennium Festival in May 2000.*
Top right: *A painting by Sunfield children welcomes visitors to the school.*
Left: *The school and its grounds today.*

A crash crop

It is now more than a century since the first motor vehicles took to our roads. And it's an odds on certainty that less than 24 hours after the first driver took the wheel the first car crash occurred. With ever more vehicles on our roads the number of cars vans and lorries being written off or requiring extensive repairs increases almost daily.

The repair of crash-damaged vehicles has been a profitable industry since the first drivers had their cars towed by horse to the nearest blacksmith to have their battered mudguards hammered straight. And throughout the course of the 20th century and into the present one the demand for such services has continued to increase inexorably - though with the kind of service being offered becoming more and more sophisticated as the years have passed.

Many readers will have had the unfortunate experience of being involved in a crash which has led to their car being taken away, never to be seen again, the only outcome eventually being a cheque from the insurance company. But what happens to the written-off vehicle, who took it away from the crash site and do insurance companies maintain huge yards full of damaged vehicles? The answer is of course that insurance companies do not keep such yards, nor do they own large fleets of recovery trucks but instead contract with specialist firms who do. One such firm which has gained a national and international reputation for its services in the field of recovering and disposing of damaged vehicles is Stourbridge-based Hewitt International Salvage Management Ltd.

Hewitt International Salvage stems from a business founded in 1945 by John Dennis Hewitt; until then he had been regular soldier, having joined the army six months before the second world began in 1939.

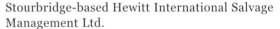

Above: *The first burnt-out vehicle recovered.*
Below: *The fleet at Himley Hall (increasing daily).*

Above: *The Junction Road site in May 1999.*

John Hewitt was born in Hagley in 1920; his father, who had been an Admiral in the Royal Navy, had died when he was two, following which John's mother had remarried. In the army John became a tank commander. John's military career was however to be cut short when he was blown up in South Africa. His injuries were horrific and would have killed a lesser man; John suffered a broken back, loss of memory and a badly damaged arm which was almost amputated; the arm was only saved by putting it in a cast with live maggots to eat away the rotten flesh; the arm survived, although covered with horrendous scars.

Returning to civilian life with no trade, John at first drove a truck at RAF Hartlebury. But that was not good enough for him. On the train journey home from the war he had met a self employed businessman in the carriage and, having engaged him in conversation, John was filled with an enthusiasm for setting up his own business.

John Hewitt became a man with both a vision and a mission. He took a belated apprenticeship with the firm of Barrington Coach Craft and simultaneously started his own repair firm. John became a workaholic, trying to build up own business whilst working in Barrington's bodyshop. Getting started at the close of the second world war was not easy, John had little funding and with few cars on the roads to be repaired, coupled with a shortage of raw materials and resources, initial progress was slow. For John a typical working day became 7 am to 6 pm at Barrington Coach Craft, 6 pm to 10 pm

was spent working in his own workshop, 10 pm to midnight was passed working from a taxi rank whilst midnight to 2 am found John working at a sandwich bar on the ring road. Not surprisingly many nights found John asleep on recreation ground near his house, too exhausted to get all the way home. No doubt his wife Lillian, whom he had married in 1944 after meeting her when she worked as wages clerk at transport company, despaired of her husband who must have seemed to her like a man possessed. But the hard work would pay off eventually.

John Hewitt's original business was simply vehicle body repairs and was started in a lean-to in Witton Street; he was soon able to rent a better building in Queens Road from the owner of the County Express newspaper and later moved the bodyshop to Wollaston. In 1962 the bodyshop business moved to Bridgnorth Road, Stourbridge where it remains today.

Three generations of the Hewitt family would eventually be involved in the business: John Hewitt's sons Paul, Mike and Adam would join the

firm in, respectively, 1962, 1965 and 1978. Mike's son Russell now represents the third generation having joined his father and uncle in 1997. The original body shop business was sold in 1986 to Paul Hewitt, who now operates independently of Hewitt International.

John Hewitt retired from his firm in 1977 although even then he could not quit working. John's hobby

Above: *A recovery vehicle from the 1970s.*
Top: *Wollaston Road site in 1999.*

was Moto-cross and between 1975 and 85 he had three moto-cross bike shops and became one of the first people in the country to import Putoline oil.

At the age of 70, in 1990, John Hewitt went to live in Spain; his sister Pauline went to live with him and she still lives there with her daughter and son in law. John continued to travel back and forth from Spain however - he was a Grand Prix motor race fan and would always come back for motor sport despite declining health and advancing age - his sons tried all kinds of excuses, with limited success, to keep him from going back to Spain. Sadly John Hewitt died in 1997.

Following John Hewitt's retirement, the business had expanded, beginning in earnest in 1986 after Mike and Adam Hewitt started working together to build up the salvage side of the company. Today about 60 vehicles move out of the company's premises each day and the firm has become the largest privately owned salvage company in the country with 23 specialised transporters collecting damaged vehicles from all over Great Britain and Europe.

The main business today is motor salvage; the firm collects and arranges the sale of damaged and salvaged vehicles from mainland UK and Europe with its customers being body repair businesses and small to modest sized salvage dealers. Most importantly however the firm now has large salvage contracts from leading insurance companies.

More recently auctions have been held every two weeks of both cars and commercial vehicles, with the latter forming an increasingly large part of business- 130 vehicles have been sold at a single auction. The auctions have been running since 1999. Today the firm has 32 employees spread over three sites: the Wollaston Road head office; Junction Road and Folkes Road, Stourbridge.

International Salvage Management aims to provide excellent working partnerships with specialist supportive attention, remaining loyal to its mission to provide a high standard of response which exceeds customers' expectations at all times, and striving to improve the quality and expertise of its service, whilst successfully maintaining its reputation for honesty, integrity and 'cultural fit'.

It is the symbiotic relationship with insurance companies which is the key to the company's success with an entire salvage management administration service being offered to clients. The firm offers a huge range of services to insurance companies including nation-wide collection of damaged vehicles, free storage facilities, the return of vehicles where requested, the disposal of burnt out or crushed vehicles and the return of tax discs and personal belongings to owners. In addition the firm offers facilities for insurance companies' own engineers to inspect vehicles, 24 hour emergency contact numbers and all backed by more than a half a century of experience in the salvage industry.

Today John Hewitt's successors aim to expand their business, buy more premises, gain more contracts and employ more people. And with Mike Hewitt having another son still at school and Adam Hewitt also having three young children the chances are that future generations of the Hewitt family will be recovering vehicles far into the current century and perhaps beyond. Who knows what that future may hold; perhaps Hewitt International may one day become Hewitt Intergalactic? Far fetched as that may sound it is a real possibility, and it is surely something which would not have been beyond the imagination of John Dennis Hewitt, a man whose unflagging ambition to reach for the stars in the 1940s and 50s made today's thriving business possible.

Top left: *A specialist slide bed recovery vehicle.*
Top right: *One of the firm's new six car Scania transporters.*

Filtered for excellence

All of us are familiar with filters, be they in coffee percolators or our water supplies. The need to reduce or remove unwanted elements from liquids is as old as man. But our small domestic needs fade into insignificance when compared to the problems faced by industry which may be dealing with millions of gallons of liquids rather than mere cupfuls. Scale and dirt can cause havoc when they penetrate control valves, turbines or other critical items of equipment. Dirt lodging in valves will cause leaks; it can also cause serious malfunctions in automatic equipment or, collecting in pipelines, will obstruct flow. When millions of pounds are tied up in plant and equipment firms naturally want to be certain that they are protecting their investment in every possible way. Firms aim to keep expensive down-time to an absolute minimum and prolong the working life of their equipment to the maximum; to succeed in that aim however they need to ensure that their pipelines are not carrying a hidden menace.

The water and oil industries in particular need to ensure the purity of their products and to do so need to make use of filtering equipment vastly more sophisticated than most of us can readily imagine. A Stourbridge company which has been successfully meeting the needs of industry in this highly specialist field for more than 40 years is Vee Bee Ltd, based in Old Wharf Road.

The firm's products fall into two main categories: cast construction and fabricated construction. The products are used to remove 'contaminate' from a wide variety of media. 'Contaminate' can range from hard hats, hammers and welding equipment left inside a pipeline after construction, down to particles so small that if they were any finer they would need a cigarette filter to remove them.

The company was founded on 4th June 1957 by William Vickery Bradley under the name Filtration and Valves. The original business activity was exactly what it is today - the design and manufacture of filtration and separation equipment.

William Bradley was born in Kingswinford, Staffordshire and started his working life as an engineer at AJS Motorcycles in Wolverhampton. Prior to starting the business William Bradley had worked for Handy Angle (now Link 51). Helped by his wife, Rose, who was involved with administration manufacture and entertaining, William set up his business at Endurance works, Maypole Fields, Cradley Heath.

Above left: *William Bradley.*
Below: *An exhibition from 1969.*

The fledging firm would spend only two years at Cradley Heath before William bought out his partner and moved to the Roetan Industrial estate in Lye. At the time the firm had just three machines and three staff; and only 1,500 sq ft of the 5,000 sq ft of the premises were occupied at the beginning. Even those premises would however eventually prove insufficient due to the rapid expansion it experienced. A further site was developed at Bromley Street industrial estate in

Those early years were hard: William found himself working seven days a week for three years without a holiday. Rose would work in the factory in the early hours of the morning painting and packing products whilst William was the engineer, designer and salesman.

William was 47 years old when he mortgaged his house to find sufficient funds to launch his own business, a major risk in middle age but one which would eventually pay off handsomely. William started out with a partner making filters and strainers and in the first few years turnover was just a few hundred pounds.

Lye in 1963. In 1967 a single storey office block was built between the two premises to form an integrated complex. After 11 years at Cradley Heath however the business would eventually move to a 9,000 sq ft open-plan factory at Bromley Street, Lye, a short distance from the Roetan estate. By 1970 the number of company employees had grown to 45 and the value of plant had increased from £2,500 in 1960 to over £40,000.

Some indication of the company's growth can be seen in its turnover: in 1960 sales had been a mere

This page: *The premises in the 1970s.*

£5,000; ten years later they had topped £170,000 and a quarter of a million pounds annual turnover was in sight.

The founder's son, Michael Vickery Bradley, joined the company in 1970 working in procurement. Sadly in 1975 William Bradley died of cancer and as a consequence Michael took over as Managing Director, appointing his mother Rose as Chairman. David G Drackley also worked for the company from the age of 16 on a voluntary basis helping with design, sales and manufacture and joined the firm officially in 1964.

Vee Bee Ltd became the new name for the company in 1980 taken from the initial letters of Vickery Bradley. By 1982 the firm had made yet another move of premises to its present four ace site in Stourbridge and continued to grow. By the early 1990s the firm found itself with a workforce of 86 and an annual turnover of £4 million 35 per cent of which was made up of export - and a third of those exports were to the highly demanding Japanese market.

In June 1998 Michael retired and his son Robert Vickery Bradley took over as Managing Director; David Drackley's son Ewan also works in the company heading up Quality Assurance.

Today Michael V Bradley still sits on the Board of Directors in a valued advisory capacity, his mother is still chairman and David Drackley though now retired from the Board still works on a part time basis on Research and Development.

Though the descriptions of the products may have remained the same through the passing years both they and their production has become evermore sophisticated. In the early days the company used lathes, vertical borers, planers, radial drills and 'tig and stick' welding sets. Today CNC lathes, CNC borers, CNC machining centres and automated welding sets are used.

Above: *The maunfacture of an early example of a Vee Bee temporary strainer.*
Below: *An early workshop view.*

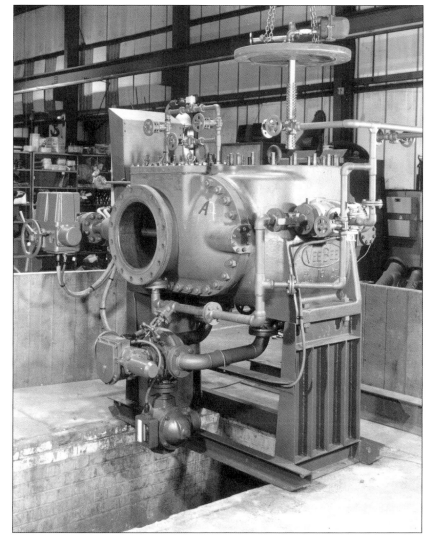

In recent times the company has spent a lot of time and money on developing its own flow testing facility which has enabled it to create many flows and operational conditions that its equipment will be exposed to in the field. This helps the firm to tailor its products to customers' exact requirements. The business is also able to use the facility to question some of the so-called facts that many have taken for granted in the past - some of the results have been surprising.

In the future the company intends to maintain a customer-focused business offering the highest levels of filtration expertise. The firm is constantly seeking to find improve-ments it can make to its current product range and for new ideas; it aims to be the recognised specialist in filtration throughout the power generation, petroleum and chemical industries world wide. In order to achieve those commendable aim the company intends to maintain its belief that the client is always right and always respond with the highest standards of service and professionalism; to continuously improve everything it does; to actively encourage open communi-cation; to constantly question and

The firm's main markets in the UK are the North Sea oil industry, the steel industry, power gener-ation, the water, heating and ventilation markets. The company also supplies overseas projects via the major contracting engineering houses in London. Main customers are the world's large oil and petro-chemical blue chip companies, all the world's large blue chip power companies and all the major engineering contractors.

The company also has a firm foothold in the Japanese filtration market and supplies oil and petrochemical companies world wide and power generation companies across the globe. It also supplies on water, plastics, chemicals and shipping contracts throughout North America, Asia, Eastern Europe, Australasia the Middle and Far East.

The firm's greatest selling point has been and remains the level of quality it offers clients. The firm always stretches itself to ensure that its products are the best that can be made. The company has a highly experienced engineering team which is always up to the challenge of finding the right solution to client's problems and is as at home with bespoke products on short turn around as it is on proprietary off the shelf items.

change to provide a competitive advantage; to listen and implement good ideas; to show appreciation for efforts and achievement; to recruit and retain only high calibre staff, to develop talent through training - and to have fun whilst working.

Above: *An automatic back flushing dual in line filter unit.* **Below:** *Finalists in the Alfred Tack Sales Team of the Year Award 1991.*

It is high summer, 1951 and these children are taking their toboggans to slide down the grass which, aided by the hot weather, was more slippery than pressed snow

Acknowledgments

Marilyn Ferris and other Library Staff at Stourbridge Library

Thanks are also due to
Judith Dennis who penned the editorial text
and Steve Ainsworth for his copywriting skills